TWAYNE'S WORLD AUTHORS SERIES

A Survey of the World's Literature

Sylvia E. Bowman, Indiana University

GENERAL EDITOR

INDIA

M. L. Sharma
Slippery Rock State Teachers College

EDITOR

Kālidāsa

(TWAS 208)

TWAYNE'S WORLD AUTHORS SERIES (TWAS)

The purpose of TWAS is to survey the major writers —novelists, dramatists, historians, poets, philosophers, and critics—of the nations of the world. Among the national literatures covered are those of Australia, Canada, China, Eastern Europe, France, Germany, Greece, India, Italy, Japan, Latin America, the Netherlands, New Zealand, Poland, Russia, Scandinavia, Spain, and the African nations, as well as Hebrew, Yiddish, and Latin Classical literatures. This survey is complemented by Twayne's United States Authors Series and English Authors Series.

The intent of each volume in these series is to present a critical-analytical study of the works of the writer; to include biographical and historical material that may be necessary for understanding, appreciation, and critical appraisal of the writer and to present all material in clear, concise English—but not to vitiate the scholarly content of the work by doing so.

Kālidāsa

By K. KRISHNAMOORTHY
Karnatak University

Twayne Publishers :: New York

Library of Congress Catalog Card Number: 77-161818

MANUFACTURED IN THE UNITED STATES OF AMERICA

Preface

The present work is designed to serve as an introduction to Kālidāsa, "the great representative of India's spirit, grace and genius." Intended as it is primarily for the general reader unacquainted with Sanskrit, controversial discussions have been eschewed and scholarly material kept to the barest minimum. An attempt has been made in this study to present the greatness of Kālidāsa in the light of Indian tradition as well as of Western criticism. The purely literary approach has not been allowed to be eclipsed by problems of scholarship. In this lies the justification of this work.

To ensure fidelity to the original, prose translations have been prepared with special care by the author to suit the needs of the general reader.

I must thank my esteemed friend and colleague in the English Department, Professor M. K. Naik, for his good offices in making this assignment possible. I must also express my gratitude to Professor Armando Menezes of the English Department in the Karnatak University, for valuable suggestions in respect of matter and diction; and also Dr. B. R. Modak, my colleague in the Sanskrit Department, for helpful suggestions.

My warm gratitude goes to Mr. Raul de L. Furtado and to Professor Sylvia E. Bowman, general editor of Twayne's World Authors Series, for their unfailing patience and courtesy.

K. Krishnamoorthy

Karnatak University,
Dharwar, India

FOR

UMẠSHANKAR JETHALAL JOSHI

WITH RESPECT AND ADMIRATION

Contents

A Conjectural Chronology of Kālidāsa's Life and Works *

Circa—		
100 B.C. or 340 A.D.		Birth
75 B.C. or 365 A.D.		(1) Ṛtusaṁhāra (The Seasons)
70 B.C. or 370 A.D.	(2) Mālavikāgnimitra (Mālavikā and Agnimitra)	
65 B.C. or 375 A.D.		(3) Meghadūta (The Cloud-Messenger)
60 B.C. or 380 A.D.	(4) Kumārasambhava (The Birth of the War-God)	
56 B.C. or 384 A.D.	(5) Vikramorvaśīya (Urvaśī won by Valor)	
50 B.C. or 390 A.D.	(6) Raghuvaṁśa (The Dynasty of Raghu)	
45 B.C. or 395 A.D.	(7) Śākuntala (Śakuntalā and the Ring)	
40 B.C. or 400 A.D.		Death

* For a discussion of this, see p. 15 f.

CHAPTER 1

Introduction: Kālidāsa and the Indian Literary Scene

I *The Age of Kālidāsa and His Genius*

KĀLIDĀSA represents the peak attained by Indian poetry in almost every genre. For over fifteen centuries, in the estimation of Indian critics as well as poets, Kālidāsa has retained his foremost place; and his fame is indeed singular in the history of India's classical Sanskrit literature. If poets of a later day begin their works with glowing tributes to Kālidāsa, literary critics and theorists have subjected his work to close analysis. His less sophisticated admirers have contributed their share of folklore and legend. One of the fables would make him a chosen devotee of Kālī, the Mother-goddess, and his poetry a sudden flow of divine inspiration. Another story would bring him the hand of a princess in marriage as a gift of the Goddess. A third would present him as an esthete among charming courtesans, finally losing his life in Ceylon through the wickedness of a mistress.[1]

Whereas these and other stories deserve to be dismissed as products of popular fancy, there is one unanimous tradition which cannot easily be set aside. It is that Kālidāsa was a court poet of the renowned emperor, Vikramāditya of Ujjain. In spite of the "discovery of Sanskrit" (usually dated 1789, the year in which the first English translation of Kālidāsa's *Śākuntala* by Sir William Jones was published) by Western scholars which has led to intense modern investigations into the ancient history of India, the veil of uncertainty surrounding the life and times of the legendary King Vikramāditya has not yet been lifted. One thing which has truly emerged from modern studies and translations[2] is that Kālidāsa's genius can find as ready a response in the Western reader as in the Indian; Kālidāsa's place in world literature is beyond question.

The consensus of Indian tradition points to a King Vikramāditya, who started an era of his own, the *Vikrama* or *Saṁvat* era in 57 B.C., after freeing the country from the menace of the Śakas. Eulogistic references to this king are scattered in some of the earliest extant Sanskrit works.[3] There are some scholars who agree that Vikramāditya, legendary patron of arts and letters, was a historical king in the first century B.C.[4] But some modern historians doubt his existence and identify him with either Samudragupta or Chandragupta II of the fourth century A.D., whose achievements are vouched for by historical evidence.[5]

What we do know is that Kālidāsa lived not later than the fifth century, since there is an inscription dated 473 A.D. which bears traces of Kālidāsa's influence.[6] One of his plays is about King Agnimitra of the Śuṅga dynasty, who flourished about 150 B.C. Some Indian scholars have suggested that Kālidāsa was a court poet of Agnimitra himself.[7]

Though in a sense it is true that Kālidāsa's date is unknown for want of records, in another sense—and that is what really matters—we are quite sure that he lived in times of peace, when the leisured class would pursue the fine arts, free from threats of invasion from without or from conflicts within. It must have been a golden age, with the king, himself a poet and artist, at the head of a court unrivaled for its artistic talents. From the works of Kālidāsa we gather that the Indian cities of Ujjain and Vidiśā were famous for their pomp and splendor.[8] In these cities, the royal court encouraged art and culture, without offending the codes of ethics and popular religion.

City life in ancient India was often sophisticated, as in certain periods of ancient Athens and Rome; but unlike the Greek and the Roman, the Indian genius had found a sort of bridge between the demands of self-restraint and self-indulgence. Within the framework of the priestly Vedic religion, there was also a popular religion devoted to worship of different gods, such as Śiva and Viṣṇu. Poetry, drama, dance, and music served not only as instruments of esthetic pleasure but also as means of divine worship. This fusion of esthetic and spiritual, of sensual and religious values is perhaps unknown, in equal measure, in any other country. Kālidāsa is the best exponent of this singularly

Indian approach to life. His imagination dwells on love which seems at first to be of the earth, but which leads imperceptibly into heavenly vistas. What appears as gross sensuality is soon transformed into domestic felicity, which culminates in divine ecstasy. This is the secret of Kālidāsa's genius, so dear to the Indian mind through the centuries.[9]

Every work of Kālidāsa—epic, lyric, or dramatic—reveals an intimate knowledge of almost all the far-flung provinces of India. The poet is as much at home with "saffron-tinted" Kashmir as with Malabar, where betel creepers entwine areca palms. His imagination loves to dwell as much on the beauty of the Himalayan heights, with their deodars and yaks, as on the colorful confluence of the rivers Gaṅgā and Jamunā.[10] Kālidāsa shows a close familiarity with the floras and faunas of the country, and also with the various strata of Indian society. He must have been a much-traveled man; it is probable that his position at a royal court was such that he could command facilities of travel in distant and almost intractable parts of the country.

The birthplace of Kālidāsa, too, is a mystery. Maharashtra, Vidarbha, Malava, Kashmir, and Bengal are some of the provinces whose claims have been seriously questioned in Kālidāsian studies. There are allusions to Kālidāsa's embassy to the court of Kuntala in the south;[11] these would indicate that the poet held a privileged status at the court of the northern King Vikramāditya.

II *Kālidāsa's Personality*

From a study of the works we can form a picture of Kālidāsa's personality. He must have been born and brought up in an atmosphere congenial to the study of both sacred lore and secular sciences like politics, erotics, and ethics. His mastery over the niceties of the Sanskrit language, with its intricate metrical patterns and rhetorical devices, points to an educational career in some learned academy at Ujjain or elsewhere. He was steeped in the lore of the land and had an insight into the metaphysical speculations of *Vedānta* as embodied in the *Upaniṣads* and the *Bhagavadgītā*. Kālidāsa had a great respect for the literature of his time, but his ambition was to create something new. The weight of learning, which is so lightly worn by him and displayed in his writings, gives the lie to the folk tales that depict him as a simple shepherd. At the same time, we notice that Kālidāsa had chosen literature as his career and was consciously mastering his diction, setting before himself the model of Vālmīki, the great poet who wrote the *Rāmāyaṇa*.[12]

It would appear that Kālidāsa was gentle and sweet-tempered, alive to beauty in nature and in the shifting moods of men and women in love.[13] He admired power and might, but only from a distance. His heroes are devoid of fury and passion. We find that he keeps steadily before his mind the twin values of *dharma* (righteousness) and *mokṣa* (enlightenment), which in literary practice lead to the ultimate mood of *śānta* (tranquillity).

It has often been remarked by modern critics that Kālidāsa ignores the problem of evil, but this is not wholly true. According to Indian ethics, the presence of evil provokes the passion of fury, and its outcome is tragedy in the case of ordinary men and women because they struggle helplessly against the universal moral order which they, unwittingly or willfully, repudiate. Such tragic heroes figure prominently in the epics and myths of India. Rāvaṇa in the *Rāmāyaṇa,* Karṇa and Duryodhana in the *Mahābhārata,* are tragic heroes. But in classical Sanskrit poetry and drama, whose aim was pleasurable instruction, the older attitude of depicting tragic characters only as foils to the virtuous heroes gained strength. The device of the deus ex machina was often used to avoid a tragic end to the lives of the good and the noble. Kālidāsa followed this convention in his works and kept out the true tragic note. Yet his imagination successfully weaves an atmosphere where even an excess of virtue becomes evil and brings upon itself the curse of suffering and doom.[14]

III *The World of Heroes*

The world of Kālidāsa's imagination is one where the heroes are models of perfection and the heroines are paragons of virtue, because they are almost divine. Yet both heroes and heroines are subject to suffering because of their unwitting transgression of the moral order. Suffering seems to purify their souls and prepares them for divine felicities. Great and noble characters, with their share of sorrow and final happiness—more in heaven than on earth—such is the universal theme of Kālidāsa's works.

The characteristically Indian belief in *karma* (action, fate) and transmigration of souls is fully represented in Kālidāsa's writings; but the people of India do not regard this attitude as a defect shutting out the tragic vision. They feel it is only a native version of the tragic vision, which emphasizes the positive "calm, all passion spent" after the storm of suffering. Nonetheless, one cannot but feel Kālidāsa's aversion to the seamy side of things. His awareness of it is part of his general philosophy, but he desists from depicting it in detail.

IV *Kālidāsa's Art*

Kālidāsa's style bears his unique stamp of perfection, whether the mood be light and gay, or poignant and disturbing, or meditative and calm. Sanskrit is a language with a vocabulary replete with clichés and with infinite possibilities for new uses of the most hackneyed words. Kālidāsa is the acknowledged master of the creative word in Sanskrit. The literary history of two thousand years does not show any other Indian poet who comes anywhere near his perfect style, in poetry or in drama. Kālidāsa's perfect *sāhitya,* or harmony, between form and content can be felt only in the original and not in translation.

If the range of Indian myths and legends, both Vedic and Puranic, serves to lend color and elevation to Kālidāsa's images, the similes and metaphors drawn from the Indian landscape create a familiar reality. They express universal thoughts and suggest more than what meets the ear. Indians value Kālidāsa most for his subtle suggestiveness, and they consider an appreciation of Kālidāsa's works an undisputed index of one's poetic sensibility.[15]

V *Order of Kālidāsa's Works*

Our uncertainty regarding the exact time of Kālidāsa's life extends also to the chronological order of his seven works: three plays, two epics, and two lyrics. Kālidāsa scholarship generally allows that the lyrics *Ṛtusaṁhāra* and *Meghadūta* represent the poet's early work, and that the epics and plays came later, *Mālavikāgnimitra* first, *Vikramorvaśīya* next, and *Śākuntala* last. Of the epics, both incomplete, the *Raghuvaṁśa* is by general consent the later one. But our treatment will follow a different order to suit a formal appraisal.[16]

The Chronology given at the beginning of the book is but a hypothetical reconstruction based on the reading of the works. Kālidāsa is assumed to have lived sixty years, either just before or after the Christian era. At the age of twenty-five he starts his literary career with the juvenile lyric, *Ṛtusaṁhāra.* He attracts the attention of the royal court by his first play, *Mālavikāgnimitra.* The prologue, however, shows that he is hesitant and still feeling his way. As a court poet and the king's friend, an unwanted sojourn in the south is forced upon him and he is parted from his wife for a year. The second lyrical work, *Meghadūta,* is an oblique record of this.

By this time he is forty years old, and thoughts of religious idealism begin to haunt his imagination. We see stirrings of this in his first epic, *Kumārasambhava,* which utilizes the ancient myth of Śiva and Pārvatī to stress the significance of self-discipline (*tapas*) as the secret of highest love. Then comes the thought of paying a tribute to Vikramāditya, his royal patron. The result is *Vikramorvaśīya,* where the semidivine hero Purūravas is, by a subtle pun, identified with his patron Vikrama.

By now, Kālidāsa has attained maturity of mind, and he essays an epic on a grand scale, the *Raghuvaṁśa.* His ambition is to present a whole pageant of national heroes, great in love and glorious in war, generous in gifts and lofty in stature; they are fired with the ideals of peace, virtue, and universal good. His initial enthusiasm, which carries him over seventeen books, receives a rude setback, perhaps from the death of his patron, and he abruptly closes with a picture of a king corroded at the core.

But the period of dark agony passes, and Kālidāsa summons up all his imaginative powers to write *Śākuntala,* his *chef-d'oeuvre.* Here his vision builds a bridge between earth and heaven, between tragedy and ideal romance, between matter and spirit. His lifework is over. Kālidāsa writes his own elegy at the end of the play: "May God decree salvation to my soul!"

The number of apocryphal works ascribed to Kālidāsa are too numerous to deserve consideration. They range from obscene verse sequences to devotional hymns addressed to various gods and goddesses. Their decadent taste reveals their spuriousness.[17]

CHAPTER 2

Three Faces of the King: The Plays

I *Sanskrit Dramatic Theory and Practice*

> Imitations produce pain or pleasure, not because they are mistaken for realities, but because they bring realities to mind.—Samuel Johnson

KĀLIDĀSA wrote three plays, and all of them have a king as hero. The variations usually noted are in the portrayal of the heroines, whose loves range from the sensual to the spiritual according to their character. Such a view, by reducing his heroes to a simple type, does less than justice to Kālidāsa's originality of conception as well as his success in dramatic execution.

A fair assessment of Kālidāsa's art is possible only in the context of dramatic theory and practice prevalent in his time. A play was meant to be staged by skilled actors. The script related only to the spoken part; the actors had to supplement it with gesture, music, and dance for the representation to be fully effective and to bring out the playwright's whole intention. The soul of a play, the pivot on which everything—plot, character, song, etc.—turns, is *rasa,* or the esthetic mood evoked in the spectators. It mattered little whether the subject was from life or mythology, whether the story was an original invention or borrowed from epic lore, whether the characters were lifelike or not. What did matter was the total appeal (*rasa*) of one dominant mood underlying the shifting movements of different states of mind.[1]

The dominant mood could be that of love or sorrow, laughter or heroism, fear or revenge, wonder or repulsion or peace. Only one of these could serve as the moving passion of a play, the rest being subordinate to it in different ways. The genius of a playwright would consist in devising a plot in which both dialogue and poetry served to release the intended *rasa* through situations which naturally fell into a fivefold division: the opening, the rising action, the climax, the denouement, and the conclusion. Indian theory indicates that a subplot or an incident should be devised to complicate the issues and to bring about their resolution in the denouement.

Indian writings have also given a detailed account of the types of heroes and heroines suited to plays of varied moods. There is a set of rigid conventions governing dialogue and description, and there is room for as many as ten dramatic forms, the best of these being the *nāṭaka,* or high drama.

All the three dramatic compositions of Kālidāsa are *nāṭakas,* and it is a primary requirement of a *nāṭaka* that the hero should be lofty and spirited, great in stature, and a model of virtue. How Kālidāsa has individualized his three heroes and how he has succeeded in contriving plots calculated to release in us the esthetic sentiment of love are questions which entail a comparison of Kālidāsa with other Sanskrit dramatists that immediately preceded and followed him.

Among the forerunners of Kālidāsa in Sanskrit drama, Bhāsa is the most significant figure. He wrote about a dozen plays, most of them being stage versions of important incidents in the two famous epics, the *Rāmāyaṇa* and the *Mahābhārata.* He showed originality in the innovations introduced by him to delineate the epic characters in a new light. Judging from his example as well as from references to the early dramas in Sanskrit, we cannot escape the conclusion that the main appeal of pre-Kālidāsian plays was religious-cum-didactic. However, Bhāsa added a new dimension to Sanskrit drama when he ably dramatized the romantic folk tale of Udayana and Vāsavadattā. Bhāsa's *Svapnavāsavadatta* is the first romantic comedy in Sanskrit, and his *Cārudatta* is the first play to introduce intrigue and social comedy in a realistic way. While Kālidāsa is undoubtedly influenced by Bhāsa in devising romantic plots with an element of intrigue, he went beyond Bhāsa in his treatment of love as a ruling sentiment. Being a more refined poet than Bhāsa, Kālidāsa introduced the lyrical element as a genuine vehicle for the expression of love in all its moods. The marriage of Bhāsa's Udayana with Padmāvatī is more a political expedient than an affair of the heart. Bhāsa is at pains to bring out the hero's loyalty and attachment to the memory of his first love rather than the frenzy of any fresh involvement.

Kālidāsa seems to have realized that the gamut of love in drama deserves a fuller treatment; that the initial stages in love must be given as much importance as love-in-separation for a full and complete presentation of that *rasa* or sentiment. From this new point of view, Kālidāsa reread his epic legends and episodes; then he chose themes that provided scope for the treatment of love in all its fullness.

How Kālidāsa's genius steered clear of the pitfalls incidental to romantic plays dealing with heroes of folklore is best realized by comparing Kālidāsa's plays with the plays of Harṣa, who succeeded him as a romantic playwright. King Harṣa (c. 600 A.D.) wrote three plays, two of which have Udayana as the hero and the third (*Nāgānanda*) has a Buddhist saint, Jīmūtavāhana, as the hero who is ready to sacrifice his love and his life to save a fellow creature in suffering. A consideration of the two Udayana plays in comparison with Kālidāsa's plays shows how Harṣa has failed in sustaining the heroic stature of Udayana. Udayana, romantically profligate to the extent of losing most of his kingdom, is not heroic enough to raise the tone of a play. The atmosphere of serious drama in Sanskrit does not tolerate any unheroic elements. This was fully realized by Kālidāsa.

Where both Bhāsa before him and Harṣa after him fail, Kālidāsa succeeds because of his discretion in the choice of his royal heroes. The kings of Kālidāsa are paragons of decorum; they are either praised in legend or cherished in history. They are all exalted personages, accomplished and cultured. After successfully discharging their state duties, they find some leisure to cultivate the fine arts. All of them are gifted connoisseurs; and they delight in the fine arts of painting, music, dance, and poetry. Much married though they be, they will yet be open to new attractions, and the intensity of their new passion is determined by the degree of difficulty in winning the beloved. In the royal harem, they observe a gentleman's code of courtesy, and they will go to any extent in appeasing the anger of jealous queens. The heroes would rather beg for their mercy than wound their feelings when caught in embarrassing situations. The jester is always there to find a way out in such predicaments. Kālidāsa's dramatic use of the jester was imitated by Harṣa in his plays.

Another important point of contrast between Kālidāsa's heroes and those of Bhāsa and Harṣa is in respect of motivation. Love can gain in dignity and intensity only if there is adequate justification for it in the lives of the lovers; it must be the result of forces that are stronger than a moment's whim or than a political expediency. Kālidāsa pays as much attention to the delineation of the different stages of love in his heroines as in his heroes. The plots devised by Kālidāsa in his three plays become meaningful only when this is realized, and in this respect we see to what extent Harṣa was indebted to Kālidāsa. Kālidāsa's Mālavikā is not just a handmaid; she is a princess in disguise betrothed by her brother to the king. She is undergoing a year's servitude buoyed with the hope of marriage with the king, a hope grounded on an oracle and on the prospect of the king's releasing her brother from the enemy's prison. But neither of the heroines in Harṣa's love plays has such a motivation linked with the prowess of the hero. Kālidāsa's Urvaśī, the divine courtesan, favors the mortal king with her love, which even the gods envy because she has been rescued by him from the clutches of a demon. Kālidāsa's Śakuntalā, too, was destined by gods and sages to marry King Duṣyanta and give him a son. Because Duṣyanta had won the favor of the gods, his son would be the first emperor of India.

Kālidāsa's greatness thus lies in having raised the tone of Sanskrit romantic drama. But for the safeguards provided by him, the Sanskrit love plays would have remained light comedies degenerating into farce. Thanks to him, Sanskrit drama remained serious and even attained a higher dignity in the hands of his able successor, Bhavabhūti.

Sanskrit drama at its best resembles Shakespeare's last plays. It could be regarded as a series of tragicomedies which have their own conventions regarding the unities of time and place. A time analysis would reveal that they try to maintain a sort of unity only within each act; sometimes several years elapse between the acts. Sanskrit dramatic practice conforms strictly to the division of a play into a prologue, five or more acts, with interludes in between, and an epilogue. While in a love play the major characters are limited to the hero and the heroine, some of the minor characters that form part of the royal entourage may play important roles in the development of action. The atmosphere of poetry, charged with imaginative power and emotional intensity, is maintained constantly during the play.

With this background in mind, we may now turn to a consideration of Kālidāsa's plays.

II *Mālavikā and Agnimitra*

(a) THE STORY. Agnimitra, king of Vidiśā, sees a new portrait in Queen Dhāriṇī's apartments and starts admiring the picture. He falls in love with Mālavikā, who is depicted in the painting as a handmaid of Dhāriṇī. Dhāriṇī, who is jealous, takes good care to keep Mālavikā out of the king's sight. But the king's jester, Gautama, is more than a match for her. When the king solicits his help, he contrives to start a big row between two dance masters in the palace, one of Mālavikā and the other of the younger queen, Irāvatī. The masters quarrel about which of them is superior and the dispute is referred to the king. The king accepts the proposal from the nun Kauśikī, also in the confidence of the jester, to decide the issue of the teachers after seeing the competitive performances of their pupils. Besides the king, Queen Dhāriṇī and the nun are to act as judges.

It is Mālavikā's turn to dance first. She executes the most difficult steps with perfect ease and beauty; her technique is brilliant, her movements are graceful. The king cannot take his eyes off Mālavikā, and, under a pretext, the jester detains her even longer than is required. The maiden's furtive glances intimate sufficiently that the king's tenderness is not unrequited.

The king is pining to meet his beloved, but this is rendered almost impossible by Queen Dhāriṇī's close watch over her. After some days, the jester finds out that Mālavikā is ordered by Dhāriṇī to be near the Aśoka tree in the park and he arranges cleverly for the king to be there. The king awaits his chance and declares his love.

But the second Queen, Irāvatī, has been an eyewitness to it all. The king had ignored her in preference to the maid! She furiously comes forward and creates a scene. The excuses of the king fall on deaf ears. Irāvatī, in league with Dhāriṇī, arranges for imprisoning Mālavikā and her friend in an underground cellar.

The jester now plays another of his tricks; he fools Dhāriṇī into believing that he is bitten by a snake and that her signet ring would help his speedy recovery. The ring thus obtained is used by him to effect the release of Mālavikā and her friend from prison, and to escort them secretly to the king who is waiting in the bower house. But here again, the tête-à-tête of the amorous couple is interrupted by the unexpected arrival of Irāvatī. A scene is happily avoided as the king has to run to the rescue of a child who is in danger of being mauled by a monkey.

When things are at their worst, several unexpected things happen. Good news comes pouring in from far and near. The king's armies have been victorious on the southern border. In the north, the armies under the command of Dhāriṇī's son have routed the enemy forces. The king's father is to celebrate this victory by performing a horse sacrifice at Pāṭalīputra, and everyone is invited to attend it. Dhāriṇī's Aśoka tree in the garden has bloomed into golden blossoms. When the queens are thus in a happy mood, envoys of the newly reinstated border king from the south are ushered in. They bring rich presents to the queens, and two maidens in the party recognize Mālavikā as their lost princess. Dhāriṇī is in a generous mood and brings about the marriage of Mālavikā and the king.

(b) THE PLOT AND CHARACTERS. The play opens with an invocation to Lord Śiva.

May the supreme Lord remove the darkness of our minds in order that we may behold the right path! Śiva is the supreme Lord conferring boundless blessings on his votaries, yet his garment is but an elephant skin. His beloved is blended in his own body; yet he is the greatest ascetic among ascetics. His eight forms sustain the entire world; yet he knows no pride!

Kālidāsa is at once characterizing his god and the hero of his play ambivalently. If the hero should appear in the play as unimperial, given to indulgence, and shorn of self-respect, one should remember that it is a pose, his real might and majesty being deliberately kept out of view.

The prologue tells us that the play is being staged for the first time at the spring festival. Also, a doubt is expressed as to how an obscure man like Kālidāsa could possibly please an audience which admires Bhāsa, Saumilla, Kaviputra, and other famous dramatists. The doubt is cleared in these words:

> All that is old is not bound to be good,
> Nor is a work bad merely because it is new;
> Scholars scan and approve of either kind,
> Only a fool is led by another's view.

Kālidāsa is confident of his powers and is competing with such masters of drama as Bhāsa. He invites critics to think for themselves before pronouncing judgment.

Bhāsa's most popular play was *Svapnavāsavadatta*. We are told in Kālidāsa's *Meghadūta* that every village elder in Ujjain was familiar with the love story of Udayana and Vāsavadattā. Kālidāsa wanted to outshine this model with a play designed for court entertainment during the gay season of spring. Udayana belonged to folklore, and his romantic adventures had passed into legend. They were recorded in what is perhaps the world's earliest anthology of folklore and romantic fables, the *Bṛhatkathā* by Guṇāḍhya. Agnimitra, on the other hand, was a historical personage. He was the son of Puṣyamitra Śuṅga, famous in Indian history as the founder of the Hindu empire at Pāṭalīputra. Agnimitra was his father's viceroy at Vidiśā, while his own son, Vasumitra, was commanding the army in charge of the sacrificial horse sent by Puṣyamitra. On the southern border of Agnimitra's kingdom lay Vidarbha, with two contending rivals to the throne.

When the play begins, one of the rivals, Yajñasena, is furious with Puṣyamitra for imprisoning the minister of the Mauryas.[2] Mādhavasena, the other claimant, seeks the assistance of Agnimitra to oust Yajñasena. Mādhavasena has a sister called Mālavikā. His idea is to give her in marriage to Agnimitra, and Mālavikā is sent to Agnimitra's court with a party led by Mādhavasena's minister.

On the way, the party is attacked by robbers, and in the skirmish the minister dies. The others, too, are lost. Mālavikā is brought captive to a border commander of Agnimitra; the commander, an illegitimate brother of Queen Dhāriṇī, sends Mālavikā to his sister as a present. The Queen, impressed by her accomplishments, employs her in her own retinue and arranges for her instruction in dancing under an expert teacher, Gaṇadāsa. Meanwhile, the minister's sister, who was also in the unfortunate Mālavikā's party, is so grieved at the death of her brother that she becomes a nun and enters Queen Dhāriṇī's establishment in the capacity of a counsellor. Her name is Paṇḍita-Kauśikī. Yet she does not divulge the identity of Mālavikā to the queen, believing as she does in the prophecy that Mālavikā would serve as a slave for one year before her marriage.

The significance of this political setting is usually missed by scholars, whose attention is directed more to the court intrigues that form the bulk of the drama. Even sympathetic critics like A. W. Ryder have found nothing much to admire in this play. Ryder observes that the play "shows no originality of plot, no depth of passion. It is a light, graceful drama of court intrigue."[3] "Criticism of the large outline of this plot would be unjust, for it is completely conventional. In dozens of plays we have the same story."[4]

The unfairness of such a view will be easily realized if we compare the plot of this play with that of Bhāsa's *Svapnavāsavadatta.* The hero of Bhāsa's play is so infatuated with the queen that he neglects his royal duties to the point of losing most of his kingdom to the enemy. The queen is persuaded, despite her profound love for the king, to accept not only a year's separation from him but also the humiliation of becoming the slave of a princess due to marry her own husband. Such a story cannot present the hero at his best. The reader's sympathy is all for the heroine. The linkup of romantic and political incidents becomes rather artificial. The second marriage of the king takes on almost the color of a marriage of convenience in spite of the author's efforts to make it appear as a love marriage.

Kālidāsa, on the other hand, takes an almost identical theme and handles it with great originality. The political issue now has nothing to do with any minister. It is the king who is in full command of the situation throughout. He has allowed himself a fortnight's holiday. In the harem, a new portrait of his first queen, Dhāriṇī, draws his attention. While admiring the painter's art, he chances to mark the beauty of Mālavikā painted as a lady in waiting. With a connoisseur's eye for beauty, he desires to meet her in person; but, knowing how jealous his queen can be, he orders his *vidūṣaka,* court jester, to arrange a secret meeting.

The jester hits upon the strategem of setting up Mālavikā's dance master Gaṇadāsa against his rival Haradatta, who has been giving dance lessons to Irāvatī, Agnimitra's second queen. He also takes the nun into his confidence, as she enjoys the trust of Dhāriṇī. The two rival masters run to the king for a settlement, and it is proposed that the relative worth of the masters can be decided only after witnessing a dance performance by their students. Dhāriṇī's attempts to stop this are foiled by the seemingly innocent nun's support of the proposal.

First, Mālavikā dances. Agnimitra, Dhāriṇī, the jester, and the nun are the judges. Mālavikā is helped by the nun to use this opportunity for winning the attention of the king. She selects a song rich in romantic associations and indicating the depth of her love for the king. The text is one actually addressed by a damsel in distress to her lover. Mālavikā's perfect figure and accomplished dance, in conjunction with this artful declaration of love, at once captivate the king. He is so swept by passion that he cannot rest.

Dhāriṇī has noticed this state of the king. She tightens her watch over the girl and decides to prevent the meeting of the lovers at any cost. In this she has the full support of Irāvatī. Though rivals themselves, they join against the common enemy.

Agnimitra, on the other hand, wants to play the ideal husband. Courtesy is his motto. He will not give the slightest offense to any of his queens. He pretends to be lost in love for each of them by turns. How to win Mālavikā's hand without offending the two queens is the problem of the play.

In Bhāsa's play, there is no development of love culminating in the second marriage; there are not even obstacles to overcome. Padmāvatī's love is postmarital. And in Vāsavadattā, the first queen, we have only what Indian critics call love-in-separation. The same is true of the agonies of grief undergone by the hero in memory of Vāsavadattā who is reported to be dead. The atmosphere of Bhāsa's play is thus charged with intense pangs of love. Kālidāsa tries in *Mālavikāgnimitra* something which is lighter in tone and at the same time truer to the spirit of the tender emotion. As Indian critics would say, the phase of love leading to marriage is the essence of this play. Kālidāsa has succeeded in inventing dramatic situations with a number of surprises which add to the liveliness of his characters. Agnimitra's philosophy of love is:

Between two in love, one ardent, one cold—
Their union by chance is not to my taste.
When both are equally ardent in love,
Even their death without union I like.[5]

This is the new philosophy enunciated by Kālidāsa as against the love of Udayana and Padmāvatī in Bhāsa's play. The innovation was so much admired by the royal poet Harṣa (sixth century A.D.) that he modeled his own plays after Kālidāsa's idea.

The background of the play provides enough scope for the growth of love in Mālavikā even before she meets Agnimitra. His charming personality inspires in her both admiration and love, and the passion burns steadily within her breast. She is only a servant in the retinue of Queen Dhāriṇī, who is more feared than loved by the king himself. Also ranged against her is Irāvatī, who is striving with all her youth and blandishments to capture the heart of the king for herself. What is more, the king, with his code of gallantry, however insincere, cannot take any positive step.

Whatever his protestations, Agnimitra cannot bear the pangs of his love for Mālavikā. He turns in his helpless condition to his jester, who discharges in this play the role of "minister in charge of erotic affairs." Perhaps in the whole range of Sanskrit drama there is no other play which assigns such a leading role to a jester, who is normally one of the conventional minor characters. The jester is the pivot on which this play revolves. He engineers all the schemes that offset the combined efforts of the queens to keep Mālavikā away from the king. He saves the king more than once from a tight spot. His sense of humor is so keen and so disarming that neither Dhāriṇī's power nor the anger of Irāvatī can disturb his peace. His loyalty to Agnimitra is complete, his cleverness unparalleled.

After his initial success in drawing out Mālavikā from the grip of Dhāriṇī to satisfy the king, the jester finds himself in a quandary. Dhāriṇī has become more vigilant. She has not forgiven the jester, nor the dance master who picked a quarrel unwittingly with his rival only to help the jester and the king in their evil designs. As for the king, he is "like a bird hovering round a butcher's shop, desirous of meat but afraid to venture."

Kālidāsa has taken pains to indicate the intensity of Mālavikā's love by providing her a friend, Bakulāvalikā, also a lady-in-waiting in Dhāriṇī's retinue. Mālavikā can share her heart's secrets with Bakulāvalikā. The ingenious jester enters into a pact with her and succeeds in encouraging Mālavikā's love for the king. Bakulāvalikā plays her role of love-messenger with consummate skill.

The turn of fortune eagerly awaited by the jester presents itself all too suddenly. Dhāriṇī injures her foot by falling off the swing. She is forced to depute a substitute for the performance of the ritual demanded by the Aśoka tree, which has failed to flower. We are not sure whether the jester did not have a hand in causing this mishap. The Indian belief is that plants can infallibly testify to a woman's quality. Anyway, the choice of playing Dhāriṇī's part in the "foot caress" ceremony designed to make the Aśoka flower falls on Mālavikā and not on Irāvatī. Kālidāsa is hinting that Mālavikā was adjudged by Dhāriṇī herself to be worthier than Irāvatī in feminine charm. Mālavikā had already come out victorious in the dance test; the Aśoka tree is the second test for her. Dhāriṇī promises to grant any wish of Mālavikā's provided the Aśoka puts forth blossoms within a period of five nights. Kālidāsa has converted a conventional and superstitious belief into a very dramatic episode vital to the climax of the play.

Both Mālavikā and Bakulāvalikā present themselves before the Aśoka tree in the palace garden as Queen Dhāriṇī's deputies. The lovelorn king is, of course, in a hurry to seize his chance. Though reminded by the jester that he has to keep an engagement with Irāvatī elsewhere in the same garden, the king is no longer sure that he can maintain his pretense of love for her. He would rather avoid the engagement because of his fear of betraying himself.

Kālidāsa has carefully prepared this scene, which is central to the play, by bringing in three pairs of characters simultaneously on the stage. Besides the king and the jester observing Mālivakā and Bakulāvalikā from behind, we have Irāvatī and Nipuṇikā watching them from the other side. The clash of interests and the interplay of emotions are very dramatic. In the conversation between Mālavikā and Bakulāvalikā we see the steady growth in the love of the one skillfully drawn out by the art of the other. This state of the sweet and gentle Mālavikā is intended by Kālidāsa as a clear contrast to the doughty and matronly Dhāriṇī on the one hand and to the irascible and jealous Irāvatī on the other. Bakulāvalikā plays perfectly the part of the king's love-messenger and promises to stand by her friend in any eventuality. In punning words she hints that the yearning of the king is identical with that of the Aśoka tree, when the king discloses himself and declares his love. Like the Aśoka tree, he is ready for her painted and adorned foot. Irāvatī, witnessing all this from behind, is beside herself with rage. Drunk as she already is, and disappointed by the king's neglect of the engagement with herself, she feels sorely insulted by the secret love between Agnimitra and Mālavikā, and angrily demands an explanation from the embarrassed king. The jester's pleas for the king's innocence fall on deaf ears. Agnimitra, at his wits' end, falls at her feet in a last attempt to pacify her. She lashes out at him, calls him a liar, and leaves him abruptly.

Irāvatī is a woman of action. She immediately prevails upon Dhāriṇī to imprison the offending Mālavikā, with Bakulāvalikā, in a cellar. The king's desires are thus frustrated by the queens. This is where the plot gets most complicated.

The king's love is now a steady flame and he cannot think of anything else. Mālavikā in prison excites our pity, but the situation seems beyond repair. Kālidāsa shows his dexterity as a playwright in making the ingenious jester perform another of his tricks. The jester learns that the guard at the cellar is authorized to admit only those who show Dhāriṇī's signet ring with the figure of a snake embossed in it. So he simulates a snakebite and, running to Dhāriṇī in the company of the king, says that he was bitten by a snake while picking a fruit for Queen Dhāriṇī. The doorkeeper, who is in secret league with the jester, brings news that the physician Dhruvasiddhi wants the patient in his own clinic and further desires a ring with a serpent's figure to effect a magic cure. Dhāriṇī, in her eagerness to save the dying man, at once offers her signet ring.

Before long, a servitor brings news of the jester's recovery, and, taking away the king on the pretext of some official duty, leads him to his summer house in the garden where Mālavikā, released by the jester, is waiting for him. For securing this release the jester outwits the guard by telling a story that the king was ordering a release of all prisoners to avert a misfortune indicated by the astrologers.

The king then thanks the jester for his labors, and the two find Mālavikā and Bakulāvalikā talking about a portrait of Agnimitra and Irāvatī on the wall of the summer house. When Mālavikā expresses her suspicions about the king's constancy, the king himself enters and allays her fears by protestations of his love. Mālavikā is more than happy, and the loving pair is left alone—but not for long.

The sight of the jester dozing like an ox on the terrace of the summer house and dreaming of Mālavikā excites the suspicions of Irāvatī, who chances to come there to see the king's portrait. Irāvatī's servant teases the sleeping jester with a curved stick, and he wakes up fearing a snakebite. The king comes out at his cry, and Bakulāvalikā appears in time to help him. Once again the king is in trouble. Irāvatī has seen through the jester's trickery and is in no mood to pardon anyone.

Only a miracle can save the king now. He cannot even concoct an excuse. Here Kālidāsa's genius invents a happy solution. Princess Vasulakṣmī, who is a little girl, is troubled by a wild monkey. Hearing her cries, the king runs to her rescue.

Mālavikā's dreams are all but shattered. Yet there is some room for hope because the Aśoka has now put forth golden flowers. Dhāriṇī has to keep her promise. Surprise upon surprise is in store for us as we follow to the close of the play. First comes the news of the victory of Prince Vasumitra over the Greeks. Secondly, Agnimitra's armies have successfully overrun the Vidarbha territory, and Yajñasena has been humbled. Mālavikā's brother Mādhavasena has been set free and has sent presents to Agnimitra through two court ladies.

It is an occasion for universal rejoicing. The bards are singing the glory of Agnimitra, who is godlike in love and war. Dhāriṇī formally invites the king to be present at her worship of the Aśoka. This is interpreted by the jester to mean an unexpected generosity on her part. Mālavikā, decked in bridal attire, is seen moving freely in the king's presence.

At this juncture are introduced the court ladies delegated by Mādhavasena from Vidarbha. They soon recognize Mālavikā as their own princess and they fall at her feet. Also revealed is the identity of the nun who offers explanations for her long silence regarding the truth about Mālavikā.

The king is supremely happy that Mālavikā has been betrothed to him by Mādhavasena. Immediate orders are passed for partitioning the kingdom of Vidarbha and installing Mādhavasena and Yajñasena as rulers of the two halves.

At the same time, Puṣyamitra's invitation for active participation in the horse sacrifice is received by Agnimitra. This train of good news culminates in Dhāriṇī's plan to unite Mālavikā and Agnimitra in happy wedlock. Dhāriṇī's promise is thus fulfilled. Even the irascible Irāvatī is reconciled, now that Mālavikā's royal parentage is established. The king's final prayer is "Oh dear Dhāriṇī, may you be ever so kind./ Nothing more is left for me to desire."

(c) GENERAL ESTIMATE. This play is interesting for more than one reason. Firstly, it embodies a philosophy of love which is characteristically Indian. Kālidāsa here appears as a spokesman for the Indian idea that love is a value no less important than religion and material prosperity. A hero is as much feared by his enemies as adored by worthy women. If Agnimitra wins the hearts of three women, each so unlike the others, it redounds to his many-faceted personal excellence. Secondly, the construction of the play, replete with surprises, is calculated to promote action. The intermingling of political with domestic issues raises the tone of the play as a whole without detracting from its primary romantic appeal. At a time when drama was still convention-ridden and concerned with only lofty epic heroes, Kālidāsa has boldly presented love in a way at once more romantic and more lifelike. The loss in high seriousness has been compensated by a gain in spirit of romantic comedy. The use of lyric poetry has been restrained and at the same time made more purposive. The atmosphere is light without being vulgar or trivial.

It has often been argued that the *Mālavikāgnimitra* is an immature work and presumably a juvenile production.[6] Such a view fails to do justice to the consummate art and dramatic skill evidenced in the play. It would be wrong to underrate Kālidāsa's art here by standards applicable to more serious drama. Presumably, this play was first staged on an occasion of public rejoicing upon his patron's success in war as well as in love.

In characterization, Kālidāsa does not betray the uncertainty of a novice. The three women represent three types of women in love, the "gentle," the "mature," and the "accomplished." It is only at first sight that Mālavikā appears passive and retiring. A closer scrutiny will show her as the ideal of a heroine in love. Her courage is seen in braving through many a mishap before and after coming to Agnimitra's court. Her silence is deliberate, and her passivity is due entirely to circumstances beyond her control. She has passed through different stages of love and is even ready to die for love's sake. Similarly, Dhāriṇī appears throughout as the mistress of the women's apartments. Her power is unchallenged, even by Irāvatī, the more youthful and buoyant spouse of Agnimitra. The king is at pains to humor her at any cost. If the combined efforts of Dhāriṇī and Irāvatī come to naught, it is due in part to the ingenious maneuvers of the jester and in part to the sudden turns of Mālavikā's good luck, but also, in a greater measure perhaps, to the unsuspected complicity of the nun.

To modern taste the play might appear slight, soft, even flimsy. But the taste of the time welcomed a treatment of love which, without being either tied down to the real or bordering on the incredibly unreal, was esthetically satisfying.

Judged by these standards, the *Mālavikāgnimitra* is entitled to a high place among Sanskrit dramas depicting *la grande passion.* It combines in the right proportions all the elements that make for popular success—painting, dance, music, sunny humor, poetry, the jester's tricks, and the element of surprise. Though within its self-imposed limits the play is a success, it cannot be classed as great drama, because it does not touch upon the deeper problems of life.

Kālidāsa has given us here an example of nature humanized. The poet's communion with nature was so complete that a mere tree becomes more than a character in the play. The Aśoka tree shooting forth flowers by the mere touch of a maiden's foot is a trite convention in Sanskrit poetry, but Kālidāsa turns this convention to true dramatic purpose. Its symbolism, too, is manifold. The Aśoka, Dhāriṇī's favorite tree, suggests in its flowerlessness her falling out of favor with the king. Its flowering out at Mālavikā's touch, on the other hand, symbolizes her good luck in love. It also bears witness to Mālavikā's blue blood.

But, more than all, it provides a chance to bring out into the garden both Mālavikā and the king. Indeed, in Kālidāsa's imagination, the Aśoka is endowed with personality.

III *Urvaśī Won by Valor*

(a) THE STORY. Purūravas, king of Pratiṣṭhāna, in answer to the cries for help from celestial nymphs, rescues one of them, Urvaśī, from the clutches of a demon after a hot chase in his heavenly chariot. The nymph and the king fall in love with each other. Urvaśī is called on duty to the court of Indra, king of the gods, but later on she manages to see the king in his garden. Complications arise as Purūravas is already married and the queen, suspecting a rival, becomes jealous.

Urvaśī has to act at Indra's court. At the question, "Who is the lord of thy heart?" while acting Lakṣmī's part, instead of answering "Puruṣottama" (Viṣṇu), she says "Purūravas." She is completely lost in her love. This lapse enrages the sage Bharata, the stage director, so much that he curses her, saying that even as she forgot her part, so would she be forgotten in heaven. Indra, however, takes pity on her and modifies the curse, suggesting that she remain united to King Purūravas on earth until he sees a son born of her.

When the queen comes to know that her rival is a nymph, she generously withdraws from the scene leaving the king free. The lovers wander together on the Himalayas when Urvaśī, seeing Purūravas' attention attracted for a moment by a charming maid at play, wanders wildly and, in a fit of jealousy, enters the sacred grove of Lord Kumāra. This grove is forbidden to women, and Urvaśī is at once turned into a creeper.

The king, in his misery at her loss, becomes insane and wanders through the forest asking every tree, stream, hill, or animal he meets about his beloved.

After many inquiries, Purūravas finds a magic gem which proves to be the jewel of restoration. Suddenly he embraces the creeper and finds himself in the arms of his beloved. They return happily to their palace.

Urvaśī is aware all the time of her curse, although the king is entirely in the dark. To put off the day of parting from Purūravas, she has deftly managed to keep her son away from his sight. Years pass and when the son Āyus is a youth, the king recognizes him by chance. Once a vulture flies away with Urvaśī's magic gem mistaking it for a piece of flesh. But, the gem is brought back by a hermit woman accompanied by a youth who had shot the vulture. The youth is introduced as his son Āyus, who was left as a child in the hermitage by Urvaśī.

Urvaśī must return to heaven, now that the son is recognized. But once again Indra allows the lovers to remain together, and all ends happily.

(b) INTRODUCTORY REMARKS. If love is a sort of pastime to the esthete Agnimitra, in Purūravas, the hero of Kālidāsa's next play, love becomes a life-absorbing passion. Agnimitra is a historical king; Purūravas is an epic character, a Vedic celebrity, and a mythological hero. Agnimitra is a man; Purūravas is a demigod descended from the god Budha. Again, though he is married like Agnimitra, he has but one queen and no heir.

Mālavikā is a girl betrothed to one whom she ultimately marries after a predestined period of suffering caused by ill luck and the jealousies of rivals. Urvaśī, the heroine of the present play, is a courtesan of the gods. She is a prized beauty who accidentally meets Purūravas halfway between earth and heaven. In the earlier play, all our attention is focused on what delays the union of the lovers, but here there is no scope for obstructions. The celestial heroine can command the elements. The first queen withdraws early from the unequal contest against the nymph. Kālidāsa attempts here, for the first time in the history of Sanskrit drama, a treatment of love at once sublime and universal, and with all its sorrows and agonies. The setting, the tone, and the action are all charged with a superhuman radiance. In this play, we get a measure of Kālidāsa's mythopoeic imagination.

If *Mālavikā and Agnimitra* has an original plot almost entirely devised by the poet, the present play contains a well-known theme recast for dramatic purposes. In Vedic lore,[7] the celestial nymph chances to fall in love with the mortal Purūravas. She sets her own conditions when entreated to stay with him. For some time they live together, but the gods so maneuver the situation that her conditions are violated by the king, and she leaves her lover abruptly. The king's entreaties prove of no avail. Purūravas has nothing but suffering left for the rest of his life. Only in a later Vedic version do we hear of Urvaśī's relenting and agreeing to a night's stay with him. But the story still remains a tragic one.[8]

There are a number of versions of this story in the later Purāṇas, or collections of ancient myths and legends.[9] In most of these, the story ends in separation. Different explanations are offered for the nymph's coming down to earth; and the reason generally assigned is a curse. The blame for the separation is often laid on Urvaśī's friends in heaven. They miss her so much that they resort to wiles resulting in the hero's violation of the conditions stipulated by her.

Only in two *Purāṇas*[10] do we have a clear reference to Urvaśī's love for the hero as the basis of the curse. The two meet for the first time in the palace garden. The madness of Purūravas during the separation is also mentioned. A second curse is said to bring about this separation.

In the first collection of Indian folk tales and legends preserved in the "Ocean of Stories" we have a reference to their first meeting in heaven in Indra's garden. Here, by God's grace, there is ultimate reunion of the separated lovers. It is difficult to decide with how many of these versions Kālidāsa was familiar. What is certain, however, is that he followed none of them mechanically, but made several changes in the story to suit his dramatic purpose.

Indra, king of the gods, is brought into prominence here for the first time, Purūravas is a close friend of his, and a dependable ally in his battles against the demons. Urvaśī is far from wicked in her relationship with Purūravas. It is out of love for him that she unwillingly brings down upon herself a curse, and values the curse as a boon in that it enables her to be with Purūravas on earth. When they are parted by a mishap, she is as eager for a reunion as the hero himself.

Unlike *Mālavikā and Agnimitra*, which is full of incidents and intrigues, this play is virtually a long lyric; there is very little action. The jester is there, but his part in the drama is negligible. There is the first queen of Purūravas, whose main dramatic function is to allow the romance to proceed. The attention of the audience is thus chiefly focused on the hero and the heroine.

An essentially tragic story has been brought to a happy close by Kālidāsa's free employment of supernatural machinery. To many modern readers, such a happy ending might appear as forced and artificial. But Indian critics have nothing but admiration for Kālidāsa's treatment of "love-in-separation." While *Mālavikā and Agnimitra* pictures love ending in marriage, here we have love that grows in the beloved's absence.

(c) THE PLOT AND CHARACTERS. The play opens with this invocation:

He whom the Upaniṣads declare to be the Person Supreme, pervading and transcending earth and heaven; to whom alone the title of Lord applies in the most significant manner,* who is ever sought within by those desiring emancipation with breath control, may He, the unchanging Śiva, easy to reach by the path of devotion, bestow on us bliss supreme.

If there is any veiled reference to the plot in this invocation, it is to the personality of the godlike hero, Purūravas. He has free movement from the world of men to the world of gods. He is every inch a king, with matchless valor. The Prologue tells us that a party of heavenly nymphs is raising a cry for help on the mountain Hemakūta. Urvaśī, with her friend Citralekhā, is being abducted by a demon.

The cries reach Purūravas' ears as he rides his chariot after the sun worship. He rushes to their help, gives the demon a hot chase, and rescues the two nymphs. Meanwhile, the party of nymphs talk about the heroism of Purūravas, recognized and admired even by Indra, king of heaven.

Urvaśī, who fainted at the demon's touch, is slow to recover. But when she learns from her friend Citralekhā that she owes her rescue not to Indra but to Purūravas, her gratitude ripens into love as she is awakened to the winsome qualities of the king. They soon rejoin the party of friends awaiting Urvaśī. Meanwhile, the fascination Purūravas feels for Urvaśī deepens when Indra's army arrives for the rescue of the nymphs. The commander congratulates the king on this good turn done to his master and invites him to meet Indra in the company of

*The word *īśvara* in Sanskrit etymologically means one who is omnipotent.

Urvaśī. The king politely declines, though he is hardly able to contain his desire for Urvaśī's company.

This episode is conspicuous by its absence in all the earlier versions of the story. It was invented by Kālidāsa to provide an opportunity for the first meeting between a king of this world and the beauty queen of heaven. It is suggested that the king is as good as Indra himself, in valor as well as in personal charm.

After returning to his palace, the king's love consumes his heart, and he cannot conceal the fact from his jester-friend. Even the queen has noted the change in him and tries her best to wrest his secret through her maid. The clever maid, Nipuṇikā, succeeds in wringing out the name of Urvaśī from the jester. The king pours out his heart to him in the privacy of the garden, where the beauty of the flowers only fans the fires of his passion. Neither the presence of his dear queen nor the pleasantries of the jester can distract him from his obsession. In verse after verse, he gives vent to his overmastering passion until Urvaśī herself arrives on the scene.

Since the hero could only sigh in his desire for the nymph, Kālidāsa has contrived that the heroine should take the lead in making a second meeting possible. Urvaśī herself is so much possessed by love that she cannot have peace until she assures herself that her love is reciprocated. It is in this role of taking the initiative that Urvaśī differs from all the other heroines of Kālidāsa. Urvaśī is a courtesan; her only interest in life is love.

Kālidāsa makes her a silent witness to the king's feelings for her. For some time, thanks to her magic powers, she watches him unobserved. She is soon convinced of his love for her and lets fall a love letter in which her heart is laid bare. Hardly has the king picked it up and read it, when Urvaśī discloses herself through her friend Citralekhā, "like lightning in the wake of the cloud." But the much-longed-for meeting is abruptly cut short by Indra's order that she should get ready to act the heroine's part in Bharata's play to be staged in heaven.

Kālidāsa now turns our attention to the innocent and helpless queen. He makes capital out of Urvaśī's love letter, which chances to reach the queen's hands through the inadvertence of the jester. The queen is not like Irāvatī of *Mālavikā and Agnimitra,* and she is much more dignified than Dhāriṇī. She charges the king solemnly, hoping that her timely intervention may yet save him. But the king is too deeply involved to forget Urvaśī. So, instead of blaming him, she congratulates him on his good luck, and only blames herself for having to stand in the way. Her anger, however, though restrained, finally makes her leave the king unceremoniously, without heeding his plea for mercy. The jester is no help to the hero. Even in his foolery there is no saving wit; and he trots out stock phrases about the delicacies of food. The king is in a dilemma. His regard for the queen has not lessened; but his love for Urvaśī has increased.

The central part of this five-act play is perhaps the most interesting from the dramatic point of view. We are first introduced to the play "Lakṣmī's choice of a husband" enacted at Indra's court by Urvaśī and her party. While acting Lakṣmī's part, Urvaśī is expected to say "I choose Puruṣottama for my husband." But her mind is so preoccupied with Purūravas that she blurts out his name instead. The result is bathos, and the sage Bharata, directing the performance, loses his temper and curses Urvaśī. She should lose her divine status at once. However, Indra decrees that the curse should end when she bears a child to Purūravas.

The motif of the Curse is a device employed by Kālidāsa in almost all his works. It is a typically Indian conception, which metes out immediate punishment to the errant, often out of all proportion. The power to curse or bless is the privilege of sages and gods. In all his works Kālidāsa uses this motif in his own original way. The curse brings with it an indirect boon. In *Mālavikā and Agnimitra* the year's exile promotes the heroine's love and marriage. In this play, Urvaśī's curse becomes a blessing in disguise. It removes the only obstacle in the fulfillment of her love: her duty as a celestial dancer. Indra's decree is actually a boon.

The hurdle on earth is also removed by the extreme generosity shown by the queen. She invites her husband to the palace balcony where she would worship the moon. The purpose of the worship is "appeasement of the husband." The queen wants to make peace with the king by keeping herself aloof from the king's love affair. The king, crushed by her kindness, tries to convince her that his love for her remains unabated. But she leaves him without showing any interest in his protestations.

Kālidāsa has so arranged the scene that Urvaśī is all the

time there with her friend, an unobserved witness to the queen's solemn declaration allowing the king to love any one that returns his love. Urvaśī now feels herself free to greet the king. Purūravas is beside himself with joy and realizes that he is more than compensated for the long agony he had undergone in her absence. Citralekhā leaves for heaven, requesting the king to make her friend happy.

This analysis of incidents can hardly indicate the degree of dramatic interest infused by Kālidāsa into this central act of the play. The queen and Urvaśī are intended as foils to each other. We have in the queen a model of a wedded wife whose whole concern in life is to keep her husband happy even if it means a surrender of her own happiness. As a complete contrast to the queen, we have Urvaśī, the very law of whose existence is love. For the sake of love, she is ready to lose her self-regard, her divine status, and all. She has no patience with right and wrong. At the same time, we have the king, who is swept off his moorings. One feels that the strongest man is made absolutely weak by yielding to a woman's passion. Neither the warnings of his jester nor the claims of his queen will dissuade him from love. Just at the point where the way is clear for the lovers, Kālidāsa has managed to conceal the seeds of a gathering storm.

In Act IV the storm breaks out with all its fury. The honeymoon proves short-lived. A flimsy excuse is enough for the nymph to fly into a rage and desert her lover. All the offense the hapless king committed was to watch a fairy girl at play in the golden sands of the Ganges near their mountain resort. Urvaśī is in an unreasoning fit of jealousy. Leaving Purūravas, she unwittingly enters the forbidden grove and is transformed into a creeping plant.

The separation from Urvaśī unhinges Purūravas and he loses his reason. His imagination weaves strange fancies when he sees friends and enemies in birds and beasts, in mountains and rivers. Kālidāsa's lyrical genius is seen at its best in designing this act in the form of an opera—all song and music, laying bare the turmoil in the hero's mind, whose monologues present his mixed feelings ranging from breathless longing to an agony of disillusion. Nowhere in the history of Sanskrit drama do we find a parallel to this scene. Here is a masterly presentation of the sentiment of love-in-separation, which has won the admiration of critics all over the world.[11] Even the hero's madness, as one critic observes, "is rather a temporary exaltation than a perversion or aberration from his natural state."[12]

The lovelorn Purūravas, mad with grief, desperately addresses the cloud, the wild flowering fern, the green grass, the peacock, the cuckoo, the swan, the *cakravāka* bird, the bee, the elephant, the mountain, the river, the palmyra tree, and the stag for news of Urvaśī. Each of these reminds him of a trait in his beloved. The first delusion—of actually meeting Urvaśī—gives place gradually to the poignant realization of the hard truth. The effect is reinforced by Kālidāsa juxtaposing Prakrit and Apabhraṁśa verses[13] and Sanskrit ones, all in the mouth of the hero. This light-and-shade effect, through the method of point and counterpoint, is unique in Sanskrit drama.

The realization that it is no demon kidnapping his Urvaśī but only a cloud, is expressed in the following manner:

> Oh! this is the new dark cloud, no doughty demon I took it for. This is forsooth an outstretched rainbow, and not the bow I thought. It is only a heavy shower of rain, no volley of shot arrows. And this is but flashing lightning, and not at all my sweet Urvaśī.[14]

The tumult in Purūravas' mind is portrayed as follows:

> Perchance, she is angry and lies concealed by her divine power. But no, her anger cannot last long. Perhaps she has gone away to her home in Heaven. But how? Her love for me is so pure! Or did the demons whisk her off? No, not while I am so nigh. Alas, she has vanished out of sight! Oh what a fate, ah me![15]

This is how the rushing river produces the illusion of Urvaśī:

> These are not waves, but the knitting eyebrows of my beloved; this row of twittering birds is her jingling belt, the bubbling foam is her gathered-up raiment unfastened in her rage; she does indeed go meandering, like a stream stumbling at every step, jealous and unforgiving that she is.[16]

Here is a portrait of the stag and hind in love:

> The hind, approaching the stag, is held back by the suckling fawn, while he looks at her with an intent gaze and with his neck eagerly bent forward.[17]

These are a few of the descriptions intended by Kālidāsa to serve the purpose of creating an atmosphere of love, as a bond between nature and man. Kālidāsa is seen here at his best as a nature poet. His imagination works at a high pitch and the process of nature pulsating with life culminates in a dramatic episode. At Purūravas' touch the creeper is transformed back into his beloved Urvaśī. Thanks to Kālidāsa's poetry, the miracle seems almost natural:

This tender creeper, its sprouts moistened with rain, like her with her nether lip drenched in tears; past its season and no longer putting forth flowers, like her unadorned; with bees no longer buzzing around, like her, speechless in anxious thought; this creeper looks like the quick-tempered Urvaśī—who, after spurning me, suppliant at her feet, is since stricken with remorse.[18]

This happy turn of events is explained by Kālidāsa as due to the magic effect of a gem Purūravas found on the way while roaming about in search of his beloved. When he is about to throw it away in a mad whim, he is asked to retain it by a hermit who pities him. The longed-for reunion comes about suddenly, and after mutual explanations there is happy reconciliation. The reunited lovers return to Purūravas' capital by air.

Even at the cost of employing supernatural machinery more than once, Kālidāsa is bent on emphasizing the value of love which is realized only after going through the agonies of separation. In its raw form, attachment, however passionate, is easily distracted by petty jealousies and suspicions. This has been well illustrated in the trivial grounds for the estrangement of the lovers. To deserve each other better, they have to undergo a period of separation without even the hope of reunion!

Fate helps their reunion when their hearts are purified by the intensity of their suffering. Urvaśī becomes a creeper; Purūravas, a madman. No other Sanskrit poet or playwright has subjected his hero and heroine to such a severe trial as Kālidāsa does in this play.

The years that follow are of unmixed delight. The only want the king feels as he ages is that of a son to succeed him. Actually, Urvaśī had brought forth a son and, keeping back the news from the king, had arranged for bringing up the boy in a secluded hermitage. The reason is that her stay on earth would come to an end the moment Purūravas knew he was a father. In the difficult choice between conjugal and maternal love, Urvaśī opts for the former.

One day the gem that had led to the reunion is accidentally snatched off by a vulture which mistakes it for a piece of meat. When the king is at his wits' end, a chamberlain brings back the gem, with an arrow bearing on it the name of the archer, "Āyus, son of Purūravas and Urvaśī." Fate thus reveals the truth withheld by the nymph. The king at once sends for her and learns the whole truth. But his joy turns into sorrow at the prospect of inevitable separation and he resolves to become an ascetic in the forest. But Indra grants him another boon. Urvaśī is allowed to stay with him till his death. The divine nymphs come down to earth to celebrate the prince's consecration as the heir apparent.

It has been observed that "the incident of the boy Āyus is forced and the ending of the drama is ineffective and flat"[19] and that "the simplicity of the story does not admit of much display of character."[20] A few words of explanation may not be amiss here. *Kāma,* or love, is to the Indian not merely a physical gratification but a value of life when governed by the goal of *Dharma*[21] which is another value of life, like *Artha,* or wealth. They are all interrelated. Love becomes an end value worth the attention of the great only when it culminates in progeny as demanded by *Dharma* and follows the attainment of *Artha.*

The hero of this play is both a king and a sage. Though his love is primarily the theme of the play, his desire for a son is an essential trait of his as a sage. Without this trait he would be no more than a voluptuary. What redeems the highly sensual heroes of Sanskrit drama is their regard for social and moral values on the one hand and for individual duties on the other. Thus viewed, Purūravas will appear as lofty and noble as Indra himself, the king of gods. Every trait in Purūravas makes him deserve this divine friendship. The whole story is based on this fact.

Nymphs in Indian mythology are so many instruments of Indra to test the asceticism of sages on earth. Urvaśī is the most famous among them. A nymph's success means a sage's fall. Almost without exception, Urvaśī has always played the role of temptress set her by Indra. She has never known what it is to be tempted. When she sees Purūravas, for the first time in her life, she falls a victim to love. She has been conquered by his valor and beauty. And Indra, too, for the first time helps her in his own way to realize her love. No better tributes can be imagined to the glorious personality of Purūravas.

Polygamy was a privilege of princes in ancient India; and absolute fidelity to one's husband was expected of every wife. In such a set-up the ideal wife could only be presented as one ready for any sacrifice, even to the point of welcoming her husband's second marriage. In all his plays Kālidāsa has presented the first queens in this role, thereby raising them in the estimation of Indian audiences. In this play, too, the first queen wins the regard of her royal spouse as well as of Urvaśī by her sagacious adjustment to the new situation.

Modern critics are generally fond of comparing Urvaśī with the first queen in the play to the disadvantage of the latter.[22] They see them as foils to each other. The queen's withdrawal is usually regarded as a weakness. It is even argued that her hold over the king's heart was too tenuous to stop him from his wild chase. But this is far from the truth. The queen strengthens her hold on the king's heart by her readiness to welcome the celestial nymph as a worthy second consort. Her doubts and suspicions relate only to a time when she is not aware of the identity of the other woman. The two women are equally entitled to our regard, the one by her sense of wifely duty, the other by her irresistible though capricious beauty.

Purūravas is every inch a king, a king even in his madness. In the storms and clouds he sees only attendants waiting on his royal person. He never for once regrets his love for Urvaśī, nor complains against his respectable first queen. Unlike Agnimitra, Purūravas does not lean for support on the resources of his jester for the promotion of his love affair. He loves deeply and suffers bravely. In this lies his greatness.

Finally, we may turn to the charge that here an essentially tragic play has been spoiled by the happy ending forced upon it by Kālidāsa in deference to convention. In the first place, it is not true that Indians as a rule were unable to appreciate a tragic close. Both the Indian epics, the *Rāmāyaṇa* and the *Mahābhārata,* have an unhappy ending. In drama, too, we have stray tragedies like *Ūrubhaṅga* by Bhāsa. In several forms of drama other than the *Nāṭaka,* there is scope for characters with tragic weaknesses. But in the *Nāṭaka,* the best among all types of drama, the hero is to be depicted as near perfect; and this is the form chosen by Kālidāsa for his plays. Then, a perfect hero could be made to suffer only for a while, at the most as a victim of freakish accidents. Lasting suffering is inconsistent with the very conception of a perfect hero.

Viewed in this light, the ideal presented by Kālidāsa in this play stands out clearly; a craving for the unattainable is sure to end in despair only in the case of ordinary men. But with epic heroes like Purūravas there is no question of failure. Their conflict is not at all with fate, because they are stronger than fate. It is in this connection that the idea of a curse becomes significant. The hero is generally blameless and may not become a direct target for a curse. Yet he may not escape the consequences of a curse involving those near to him. The duration of a curse is limited, while the course of destiny is inexorable. Especially when the provocation is slight, the curse cannot be severe and the happy ending becomes inevitable. This rules out the possibility of a complete desertion of Purūravas by Urvaśī.

The character of Urvaśī as conceived by Kālidāsa is diametrically opposed to that of the fickle wanton of the Vedic story. Possibly, Urvaśī represented in the myth the vanishing beauty of the dawn. But in the play, Kālidāsa's concern is to portray only the ecstasies and agonies of love, short of death. For, by definition, Urvaśī is an immortal, and Purūravas is almost so because of his relationship with Indra. One has to admit that the play cannot stand comparison with Shakespeare's best tragicomedies, either in psychological depth or in complexity of poetic images. Yet Kālidāsa achieves a unity of dramatic tone by utilizing the triple means of poetry, music, and dance.

IV *Śakuntalā and the Ring*[23]

(a) THE STORY. King Duṣyanta of Hastināvati comes to sage Kaṇva's forest hermitage during a hunting excursion. The sage is not at home, but the king meets his foster daughter, Śakuntalā, the child of the nymph Menakā and sage Viśvāmitra. Śakuntalā is watering the plants along with two girl companions when a bee starts harassing her. The gallant king frees her from the bee and, struck by her beauty, falls in love with her. With due modesty, Śakuntalā returns his affection.

Duṣyanta prolongs his stay in the hermitage under the pretext of defending it from wild animals and demons. Both Duṣyanta and Śakuntalā are burning with intense love for each other and they marry secretly.

The king has to return to the capital and leaves his ring with Śakuntalā who is to follow him later. Kaṇva is still away and Śakuntalā is daydreaming. Meanwhile, the irascible hermit Durvāsas visits the hermitage, and, imagining a fancied slight, pronounces a curse to the effect that Śakuntalā will be forgotten by her husband until the sight of his ring given to her as a token. Śakuntalā is kept ignorant of the curse by her two companions.

Kaṇva now returns, approves of what has happened in his absence, and sends Śakuntalā to her husband's palace with a retinue of forest hermits. When Śakuntalā is introduced to Duṣyanta, he fails to recognize her as his wife in spite of her best reminders. The ring, which might have aided recognition, has been lost in a river by Śakuntalā. In her plight, Śakuntalā is pitied by her mother Menakā and taken away to heaven where she gives birth to a son.

In the meantime, a fisherman finds the king's ring inside a fish and, while attempting to sell it, gets caught by two police officers. He is hauled before the king under suspicion of having stolen it. But the king's memory is restored on seeing the ring, and the fisherman gets a reward.

Duṣyanta is now repentant and blames himself for his heartless conduct toward Śakuntalā. While returning to earth after rendering help to Indra in heaven, the king happens to visit on his way the hermitage of the divine sage Kaṣyapa. There he watches a boy playing with a lion's cub and discovers that it is his own son, Bharata. He is reunited with Śakuntalā, and Kaṣyapa frees him of his feeling of guilt by telling him the story of the curse.

(b) INTRODUCTORY REMARKS. By general consensus, *Abhijñāna-Śākuntala* is Kālidāsa's masterpiece. In 1791, it drew forth the following encomium from Goethe, who read the play in a German translation from English:

Willst du die Blüte des frühen,
die Fruchte des späteren Jahres,
Willst du, was reizt und entzückt, willst
du, was sättigt und nährt,
Willst du den Himmel, die Erde mit
Einem Namen begreifen,
Nenn' ich, *Sakontala,* dich, und so ist alles gesagt.

If you would enjoy the flowers of early years
and the fruits of age advanced,
If you want to have something that charms,
something that is enchanting,
If you want to designate both the heaven
and earth by a common name,
I refer you to the Śakuntalā and thus express
these all.

Śākuntala combines, according to the German poet, the flowers of spring and the fruits of autumn, what delights and satisfies with what uplifts and enraptures; in a word, heaven and earth itself. Rabindranath Tagore has an illuminating commentary on this encomium in one of his essays.[24] He speaks of two unions in the play, one sensuous and earthly, the other spiritual and heavenly. Another German critic, Alexander von Humboldt, is all praise for the poet "who describes like a master the influence of nature on the minds of lovers."[25] Speaking of love in this play, Dr. S. Radhakrishnan observes "passion is linked with the sanctities of life; nature and grace blend in harmony."[26]

If Kālidāsa is unanimously recognized as a world author by critics of the West it is mostly because of *Śākuntala.* The theme here is love, both in its raptures and in its torments. Duṣyanta is a superhuman king, more like Purūravas than Agnimitra. Śakuntalā is a nymph's daughter, but in character more like Mālavikā than Urvaśī. The jealous and recanting queen is very prominent in *Mālavikāgnimitra,* less so in the *Vikramorvaśīya,* and all but disappears in the *Śākuntala.* Similarly, the jester is the engineer of the King's amour in the *Mālavikāgnimitra,* an obstacle in the *Vikramorvaśīya* and almost neutral in this play. The atmosphere of the hermitage is unknown to the *Mālavikāgnimitra,* barely alluded to in the *Vikramorvaśīya,* but assumes remarkable importance in the present play. The quality of opera is broadly suggested in the *Mālavikāgnimitra,* becomes supremely important in a whole act of the *Vikramorvaśīya* (the fourth), but recedes again in the *Śākuntala.*

A comparison of the three plays reveals how Kālidāsa was introducing variations, at once subtle and profound, into his favorite theme of love. Mālivāka represents woman confident of her conquest in her own good time despite the intrigues of her rivals. Urvaśī is a model of one whose love is a boon and whose life is dedicated to nothing but sweet delight. In this play, however, Kālidāsa presents the heroine as Nature's darling, innocent as a deer and caught up in a love for a highly sophisticated man. The device of the curse is employed here to serve a dual purpose. It explains the suffering the heroine is made to undergo before the final reconciliation, as partly rooted in her nature. Also it shields the hero even when he disowns marriage with Śakuntalā. The commutation of the curse to the effect that the king's signet ring will be the means of ending the separation prepares the way for the play's happy ending.

Thus, in all the three plays, the theme, the characters, and the dramatic devices all remain more or less similar. So, too, are the supernatural and romantic episodes. The poetry breathes the same passionate intensity. Nonetheless, what makes *Śākuntala* stand out as the masterpiece it is, is the spiritualized treatment of nature, seen here for the first time, and the atmosphere of sanctity that, thanks to the sages, pervades the play. Love, depicted here as the cardinal sentiment, does not cloy by its excess. Kālidāsa, therefore, is above the charge of sentimentality which stains a good many of his imitators. Further, it is only here that Kālidāsa has been able to do justice to the rival claims of duty, prosperity, love, and spiritual good—the four Indian values of life. Finally, the greatest scope is provided here for Kālidāsa's genius to manifest his insight into the rare theme of amnesia.

This is made clearer by a comparison of the plot of the play with its original source. The episode of Śakuntalā occurs in the first book of Vyāsa's epic, *Mahābhārata,*[27] where neither Duṣyanta nor Śakuntalā show up too well in the love affair. We see more of Śakuntalā's ulterior motives, and less of her love, in her surrender to Duṣyanta. She wants the kingdom for her child and extracts from the king a promise to that effect. Similarly, Duṣyanta unbecomingly goes back on his promise and repudiates her as well as their son when they present themselves at his court. It is only by a divine intervention that he is forced to accept them. There is no scope here for exhibiting the different stages of love either before or after marriage. But Kālidāsa has totally recast this story and introduced many new elements, like Durvāsas' curse, the signet ring, with a history of loss and recovery, and reunion with wife and child in Indra's heaven. New characters, like Kaṇva, Indra, the jester, the fisherman and the police, are introduced to add to the interest of the play.

(c) PLOT AND CHARACTERS.

> May the Lord, visible in his eightfold form, preserve you—that form which is the first in creation, namely, water; that which bears ritual offerings, namely, fire; that which is the offerer, namely, the priest; those two, the sun and the moon who regulate time; that ether which pervades the universe and is distinguished by sound; the earth renowned as the womb of seeds; and finally air, that gives life to all that lives.

This invocation is at once Vedāntic wisdom and a symbolic indication of the plot. The opening song describes summer:

> The days make for a pleasant dip in water whereon sylvan breezes, fragrant from the touch of trumpet flowers, woo to easy slumbers in the shade and are most delicious towards their close.[28]
>
> Buxom maidens make earrings of dainty-tendrilled *Śirīṣa* flowers gently kissed by the bees.[29]

Like the audience carried away by the melody of the song, Duṣyanta is lost in his pursuit of a deer. Such is the short but effective introduction to the play proper provided by Kālidāsa.

King Duṣyanta has followed the deer far into the forest. His retinue is left far behind. He is about to shoot the deer with his arrow when he is stopped by two ascetics, for the animal belongs to their hermitage. The king's ready compliance draws a blessing from their lips: "May you get a son, the universal emperor of earth and heaven." They also explain that they are near the sage Kaṇva's hermitage on the bank of the river Mālinī and invite him to pay a visit to it and partake of the hospitality of Śakuntalā, the hostess, in the absence of her father, Kaṇva.

The tranquillity of the hermitage and the beauty of nature around it impress the king so much that he is fascinated by it all. He alights from his chariot and, on moving a few steps forward, finds three maidens engaged in watering plants. Their bewitching beauty draws a cry of admiration from him:

This dweller of a hermitage excels the inmates of the royal harem in her beauty even as the forest vine outshines the garden creeper.[30]

Their sprightly talk rouses his curiosity, and he draws near to listen to their guileless conversation. He soon realizes that the fairest of them is Śakuntalā, and the other two Priyaṁvadā ("the sweet-tongued"), and Anasūyā ("the unenvious"). Her garments, woven of simple bark, cannot conceal Śakuntalā's beauty from the trained eyes of the king:

The lotus in the pool is lovelier for the weeds that beset it. The dark spot of the moon adds to its comeliness. This slender maid is the lovelier for her bark-garment. What then is not an ornament to forms by nature sweet?[31]

The maidens are talking about the marriage of vines with trees, as if they were their sisters and brothers. The subject of Śakuntalā's marriage comes up casually. The king is wondering whether Śakuntalā is worthy of him by her birth, but he soon reassures himself that, righteous man that he is, his instinct can never go wrong.

Duṣyanta comes out of hiding with the excuse of driving away the bee which is teasing Śakuntalā. By slow degrees the maidens are made to realize his identity. On the other hand, he too gathers several details about Śakuntalā's life, which confirm his earlier intuition. As a token of his feelings toward Śakuntalā, he shows them his signet ring and retires. Enough indication is given of the genesis of natural love, each finding in the other the ideal come true.

Kālidāsa has thus pictured Śakuntalā as a fine flower of nature, a nymph's daughter brought up by a sage, so combining in herself romantic beauty and ascetic simplicity, artless charm and conquering passion. The playwright has also very subtly shown that the paradox of passion in a grove dedicated to penance contains within itself the seed of tragedy. There is a clear allusion to the gathering storm, unknown to the guileless girl, but within the knowledge of the all-wise Kaṇva. Kaṇva's absence from the hermitage is calculated to mitigate her inevitable fate. It is in this connection that the details of Śakuntalā's birth gain more meaning. Śakuntalā is a child of the nymph Menakā who had once come to tempt the sage Viśvāmitra out of his vow of celibacy. In Śakuntalā's blood there runs a conflicting strain bound to bring about a crisis but, thanks to the spiritual forces at work, with the certainty of a happy ending.

In deference to Indian dramatic theory that the erotic is best promoted by association with the comic, Kālidāsa introduces the jester in the second act. However, in view of the serious turn the plot has to take, he is whisked away when the act closes, not to reappear until Act VI. The jester is seen complaining about the hardships of camp life, raving against hunting, and pining for the royal cuisine. But his friend, the king, is in no mood to return early as his heart is stolen by Śakuntalā. The king cancels the hunting excursion despite the importunities of the general to pursue it. The more the jester tries to dissuade him from his incomprehensible infatuation for a hermit girl, the more eloquent the king waxes about her peerless beauty. The main interest of the scene lies in their conflicting purposes—the king seeking the jester's help to prolong their stay in the hermitage, and the jester pressing the king all the time for a quick return to the city.

Kālidāsa resolves the problem by a deft invention. There is a deputation of the hermits calling on the king to prolong his stay and protect them from the menace of demons. The king's decision is rendered difficult by the simultaneous message he receives from the queen-mother that he should be present at the religious function arranged by her in order that he may be blessed with a son. The king is in a dilemma, but only for a moment. He asks the jester to be his deputy at the religious function so that he can accede to the request of the hermits.

There is a problem though. The king would not like his secret let out in his harem by the loose-tongued jester. So, before they part, he makes a spirited disavowal of his interest in Śakuntalā. He declares that he was only jesting all along and that the real reason for his staying behind is nothing more than protecting the hermits, which should have precedence over all other duties. The whole hunting retinue is sent back to the city along with the jester.

A fortnight has passed when Act III opens. The king is still in the hermitage guarding the hermits, and biding his time to propose to Śakuntalā. Since their first meting, Śakuntalā has been lovesick. Her friends see no improvement in her condition in spite of the best treatment known to them, as she is too shy to disclose the real cause of her illness. But at last they succeed in drawing out her secret.

Meanwhile, Duṣyanta, who is close to the scene, happens to overhear the much longed-for confession of love from his beloved. He congratulates himself on his good fortune. He cannot understand why Śakuntalā should doubt his own eagerness for her:

A seeker after Fortune may or may not come by her. But where is the man who will reject her if Fortune herself come seeking him?[32]

Encouraged by her friends, Śakuntalā writes out her confession in a quatrain, but even before it is delivered, Duṣyanta presents himself and sets her fears at rest by his reassuring protestations of love. As a token of his genuine love, the king gives her his signet ring and promises soon to take her to his palace as his favorite queen. The two are left alone for a few moments. Though Duṣyanta has to leave suddenly to punish the demons, Kālidāsa suggests that the initial fears and suspicions on both sides have been overcome, leading to their secret marriage.

The progress of love outlined in this act is calculated to conform to Kālidāsa's ideal of love which we already saw in *Mālavikā and Agnimitra*: one-sided passion, however intense, is not to be mistaken for love. Love springs only after there is sufficient proof that the other yearns as much for union as oneself does. In this connection, we may notice some of the charges leveled against Kālidāsa by some modern critics. "The great problem that Kālidāsa set before him in writing this drama was to trace the development of earthly love into heavenly love, of love that is self-centered into love that is universal."[33] "Śakuntalā, the youthful maiden of Kaṇva's hermitage, needed the external token of recognition and she banked upon its use in case Duṣyanta did not recognise her. What a commentary upon the fickleness of that love which required such extraneous visible signs for its avowal!"[34]

The first critic characterizes the boundless love of the couple for each other depicted in this act as earthly and self-centered. This is to misunderstand Kālidāsa, whose idea of love in the three plays is all of a piece: "the red-hot iron welds only with another equally red-hot." Its whole and sole justification is the prompting of the heart. Until each is prepared to wait for the other to give indications of mature love, there is no love at all. Sensual passion and poetic love are thus clearly distinguished by Kālidāsa. Hence, there is no justification for the allegation that we have in this act anything like earthly love contrasted with heavenly love.

The second objection, that love that demands proofs like a token ring ceases to be genuine, is a distortion of truth. The bride is answerable not only to herself but also to her parents in the choice of her life mate. Particularly when the parent is absent, she has to make doubly sure that her choice is worthy. From this point of view, the token and the promise become necessary as solid proofs to convince her parent if not herself. On the other hand, we cannot forget that Duṣyanta also had his initial misgivings about the suitability of the maiden. All this points to Kāliḍāsa's intention to present ideal love as one governed by moral standards. In fact, as we shall presently see, the central problem of the play hinges upon it. Act IV is central to the play not only by virtue of its position but also by its degree of interest as judged by the Sanskrit critics. Here we do not have much action, except for the momentous incident of Durvāsas' curse. We also meet for the first time Kaṇva, who approves of Śakuntalā's secret marriage, congratulates her on her wise choice, and makes all the preparations for sending her to Duṣyanta's palace. The leave-taking scene is very dear to the heart of Indian critics. Kaṇva's grief at parting from his dear daughter is poured out in verse after verse, exquisitely tender and moving.

Even before the act opens we are introduced, in the interlude, to the proverbially irascible sage Durvāsas who pays a casual visit to Kaṇva's hermitage in his absence. Śakuntalā, who is brooding over her love and wondering why the king has not sent for her even after three weeks, does not notice the presence of Durvāsas at the door and fails to extend to him the expected welcome and hospitality. Unfortunately, her friends are not at hand either. The sage flies into a rage and utters a curse: "May he, doting upon whom you are neglecting me, forget you altogether. May he not remember you even when reminded."

When the friends find him walking angrily away, they fall at his feet and beg for mercy. The sage relents and decrees that the curse will cease to work when the king sees the signet ring. The friends are happy that the remedy is within easy reach and decide not to tell Śakuntalā anything in view of her delicate condition.

Kālidāsa has with great effect employed here the device of dramatic irony. While the audience is aware of the impending misfortune, the victim herself is ignorant of it. If Kaṇva, in his infinite wisdom, has glimpses of it, he keeps his own counsel and plays the part of a humane and thoughtful father in bidding farewell to her with only high hopes and best wishes for her welfare. The innocent Śakuntalā claims our sympathy most, as much by her buoyant spirits at the prospect of joining her husband, as by her tears at having to leave her dear father and long-cherished home.

Śakuntalā is with child. Her friends have been worried as to how this could be disclosed to Kaṇva on his return. But the problem is easily solved for them by Kaṇva's own keenness of observation and wholehearted approval of the marriage. On the day of Śakuntalā's departure the whole hermitage is busy, the elders with their blessings and the friends with her makeup. The very trees of the forest are said to present to her rare ornaments required for the occasion.

Kaṇva is overcome with boundless sorrow as the hour of departure draws near. It finds expression in verses regarded by tradition as some of the best in the whole drama:

At the thought that Śakuntalā will go away now, my heart is smitten with melancholy, my throat is choked with tears and my eyes are heavy with care. If such be the grief of a forest dweller like me, how much more should householders* be troubled by the unwanted grief at parting from a daughter?[35]

(Oh trees!) She who would not dream of drinking water so long as you were not watered; she who, though fond of ornaments, would not, for love of you, take a shoot from you; she for whom your first

*The Sanskrit original is *gṛhiṇaḥ* which means a head of the family responsible for the welfare of his wife and children.

blossoming was a festive occasion—even that Śakuntalā is going away to her husband's house. Do you all say good-by to her.[36]

Kaṇva has an advice for Śakuntalā:

Attend upon your elders; conduct yourself as a dear friend towards your fellow wives; though wronged by your husband do not be cross with him and sulk; be most considerate toward your dependents, and not arrogant in your prosperity. Maidens thus attain the status of mistress of the house; those who do not, are the family's curse.[37]

For Duṣyanta Kaṇva has a message:

Pay due regard to us whose wealth is austerity; consider well your own exalted lineage; remember also what love this girl bears you, free, not prompted by her kinsfolk. It behoves you to regard her among your queens with equal honor. The rest depends on fate; and it is not for the bride's relations to dictate.[38]

In this leave-taking scene Kālidāsa achieved an operatic effect by the use of melodious and harmonious metres to describe the vine, the deer, and other inmates of the hermitage, all plunged in the grief of separation. It is the universality of pathos which makes the act so successful despite its want of dramatic action.

We now come to Act V, which represents the climax of the play. At the very outset, we get a glimpse of King Duṣyanta's daily routine. Dedicated to the welfare of his subjects, he has little time for recreation in the harem. Queen Haṁsapadikā is singing a love song hinting at his neglect:

O bee, after you have kissed the mango blossom all over, how is it that, in your fancy for fresh honey, you have all forgotten her, and are content to rest in a lotus?[39]

The gallant king is quick enough to see the point. But the music only fills his mind with a melancholy he cannot understand:

When a person, though happy, on seeing things beautiful and hearing sweet sounds, becomes full of longing, then, perhaps unwittingly, he is recalling in his mind the love ties of a former birth, rooted deep in his being.[40]

The background for the climax is thus deftly suggested. The theme of amnesia is subtly introduced. Does it point to a flaw in Duṣyanta's character? Many a critic has felt so. "In passing from the fourth Act to the fifth we suddenly enter a new atmosphere; from the ideal world of the hermitage we go forth to the royal court with its hard hearts, crooked ways of love-making, difficulties of union."[41] The criticism is unfair. We cannot judge a highly imaginative romantic and opera-like play by the standards of realist drama. The poet's intention is to show how devoted the king is to his first duty, even at the cost of misunderstanding. A virtue from one point of view may appear as a blemish from another. Unlike the other two plays, we have nothing in this to warrant the conclusion that Duṣyanta was fickle. His two queens are but names in the play. They do not even make an appearance on the stage. The question of their coming in the way of the king's plans does not arise. While studying this play, we must accept the convention that the king was entitled to have more than one queen. We should not also forget that Durvāsas' curse is already set in motion.

When the arrival of Śakuntalā and her suite of hermits is announced, the king respectfully offers to receive them in the hall of fire worship. After the initial greetings, Kaṇva's pupils, Śārṅgarava and Śāradvata, convey Kaṇva's message to the king: "You are surely the best of worthy men. Śakuntalā is like a good deed incarnate. By uniting a bride and groom of equal virtues, the Creator is at last exempt from blame. It befits you to take her, enceinte as she is, to fulfill your duties as householder."

The king is in a quandary. However hard he may try, he cannot recall his marrying Śakuntalā. Politely but firmly he says as much. Kaṇva's pupils fly into a rage and rudely call him to order. The old hermit woman in the suite suggests that Śakuntalā unveil her face to help the king recognize her. The king finds her beauty fascinating enough to take her for his wife, and yet he asks Śārṅgarava how he could ever take a pregnant woman into his harem. How could he confess himself an adulterer? The hermit can only refer him to Kaṇva's words, which, however, fail to convince the king.

As a last resort Śakuntalā herself addresses the king in the name of justice. She is, however, asked to produce proofs. She is on the point of showing the signet ring when she discovers its loss. Apparently, it had slipped off while she bathed in the river on her way to the palace. Desperately, Śakuntalā recounts some of the most intimate talk they had had together in the hermitage. But all is in vain. The king calls her a cunning female and a liar.

At this Śakuntalā is so incensed that she calls him a vile man, hiding a vicious heart under a gentleman's garb, even as a treacherous well covered over with grass. Her vehemence leaves the king perplexed for a moment. But, on second thought, he remains firm and succeeds in convincing the hermits that he gains nothing by deceiving a woman and that his stand is dictated only by considerations of his royal duty. The hermits depart, leaving Śakuntalā to her fate.

The king's chaplain suggests they might keep her in the palace till her delivery. Perhaps the baby's looks will decide the issue for good. Meanwhile, there is a lightning flash and Śakuntalā vanishes into the heavens held by Sānumatī, a goddess dispatched by Śakuntalā's mother.

More often than not, Duṣyanta's character in the above scene has been misjudged. Excessive sympathy for Śakuntalā in her plight might incline us to judge Duṣyanta more severely than he deserves. Kaṇva's pupils, to whom the city itself is no more than a hotbed of chicanery and fraud, expose their own prejudice in their quick condemnation of the king. Kālidāsa has taken pains to redeem the king from the charge of fickleness and heartless deception which he found in his epic source. There is a conflict in his mind between his certain duty to his state, and an uncertain choice, though the bait set before him is a matchless beauty ready to be his wife together with the prospect of an heir to the throne. The guileless nature of Śakuntalā and her entourage, as well as their outspoken talk, make him doubt his own stand. This complete loss of memory, once granted, makes his action quite blameless. It is a hard test imposed by fate on both Duṣyanta and Śakuntalā, and they emerge all the better for it.

Fate is a potent force in this play. We have many allusions to it scattered throughout. Kanva's absence from his hermitage to mitigating it by exceptional austerities, Śakuntalā's consent to a secret marriage, the unaccountable loss of the marriage token, the unfortunate fact that the jester, not having seen her before, could not vouch for her now—these are some of the strands that fate has woven. Durvāsas' curse is but a corollary of this inexorable fate, not its cause. Any hope of reunion is possible at all because the king is so righteous and the heroine so innocent, and there is still faith in justice. The idea of Śakuntalā's sin, with retribution overtaking her, is no more than an imposition by Tagore with no textual support.[42]

A word about the supernatural element employed by Kālidāsa in this act: if we remember that there is a mythological plot with semidivine characters, the sudden appearance of a goddess to rescue the desolate Śakuntalā may not seem a failure of dramatic probability. On the other hand, it sows the seed of hope for an eventual just and happy solution.

In Act VI we are introduced to two important incidents setting the process of denouement in motion. The ring is found by a fisherman in the belly of a big fish. He gladly takes it to the city for sale, only to be caught by the police and taken before the mayor. Seeing the king's name engraved on it, the mayor sends it to him. Fortunately, the fisherman's story is confirmed by the king who orders a reward for the finder.

The king's memory is fully revived at the mere sight of the ring. He recalls every minute detail of the sweet hours he had spent with Śakuntalā. His remorse now is as complete as his former forgetfulness. He feels he has himself to blame for all the misery, and all the jester's efforts at comforting him are in vain.

As an eyewitness to Duṣyanta's self-condemnation and eagerness to undo the evil, Kālidāsa has brought Sānumatī herself, Śakuntalā's friend now in heaven. Her report to Śakuntalā of Duṣyanta's change of heart is calculated to sustain her drooping spirits. Though the hero and the heroine are still unaware of the curse, the audience can look forward to a happy ending.

In his anguish, Duṣyanta has banned all festivities from his palace. He turns to the painter's art as a means of diversion and paints the portrait of his beloved, with the Himalayan range as a backdrop, in the natural setting of the hermitage on the banks of the Mālinī, with swans and deer sporting about on the sands. He is so dispirited that he cannot discharge his state duties. He has ordered that important appeals be brought to him in writing. One of them is concerned with confiscating the property of a merchant who had died heirless. The king's heart has been so softened by his folly of disowning his own heir that he decides to transfer the property to the posthumous child to be born of the widow.

Sānumatī, who has witnessed this incident too, returns to heaven, doubly confirmed in her opinion of the king's change of heart. The act closes dramatically, with a sudden cry for help from the jester. Rushing to his rescue, Duṣyanta finds that it is only Indra's charioteer sent from heaven. The charioteer asks the king to go with him in the chariot, to help his friend in his battle with the demons.

From Sānumatī's reflexions on seeing the repentant king we gather how Śakuntalā is constant in her love for Duṣyanta in spite of his rebuff. Now that Sānumatī has seen Duṣyanta's real nature, she comes to appreciate Śakuntalā's singular attachment to him. Tagore declares in this connection that deep grief made Duṣyanta renounce the role of a rake; and how "Kālidāsa has burnt away vice in the eternal fire of the sinner's heart."[43] All this, couched in figurative language though it is, fails to interpret the true intention of Kālidāsa who was himself more of an esthete than a moralist.

In the last act we meet Duṣyanta in heaven. He has won the battle for Indra and is on his way back home. Attracted by the tranquil atmosphere of the sage Mārīca's hermitage, Duṣyanta alights for a while:

> There stands a sage still as a tree trunk, facing the sun's orb. His body is half-buried in an anthill. Sloughs of snakes cling to his breast, and his neck is choked by tendrils of ancient creepers. His hair, which spreads over his shoulders, is all a matted mass filled with birds' nests.
>
> His sustenance for life is drawn only from the air; the place is a grove full of wish-yielding trees. Here sacred ablutions are done in waters yellowed by the pollen of golden lotuses. Here, on jeweled slabs meditation is practiced and, in the presence of celestial nymphs, ascetic austerities. Thus these sages practice penance, surrounded as they are by what are rewards of penance for others.[44]

This is the second hermitage in heaven which has drawn encomiums both from Goethe and Tagore. It shows how Kālidāsa's heart is in tune with the ascetic ideal upheld in India. This ideal is not the gospel of the indigent, but a positive value to be striven after even by those who have all their earthly wishes fulfilled. An index of the peace and tranquillity reigning in the hermitage is seen in a six-year-old boy playing happily with a lion's cub sucking its mother's milk. The boy is naughtily forcing its mouth open and counting its teeth.

Duṣyanta's heart overflows with affection for the boy. He tries to draw him away from the cub by promising him other things to play with. The maids in charge are outwitted by the boy, and the king's words too fall on deaf ears. Gradually, Duṣyanta discovers royal marks on the boy's palm. The maids too are struck by the similarity in features between the two. When asked about the boy's father, the maids have nothing more to say than that he is the one who disowned his wife. The mother's name, casually mentioned, turns out to be Śakuntalā. Duṣyanta is sure that the boy is his own son.

Kālidāsa has here composed a scene tense with suspense and surprise. Duṣyanta's heart, pining for Śakuntalā, gets a foretaste of joy by this meeting with his son. Śakuntalā, too, is brought on the scene by the maids' report that the boy's father has arrived. The boy's talisman had not turned into a snake when touched by the stranger. As the boy is turning away from the stranger, he is surprised to see his mother's courteous attitude toward him. She will not listen to his apologies. So eager is Śakuntalā for reunion, that she no longer wishes to wear his fateful ring when he presents it to her anew.

Meanwhile, the charioteer who had been to the sage to make an appointment, is back. All three hurry to meet him. The all-knowing sage blesses them and, to console the penitent Duṣyanta, declares it was not he that was to blame but Durvāsas' curse. He also prophesies that the boy will be the first emperor on earth. The sage Kaṇva, he adds, knows all. This reunion of the three is likened to the perfect union of piety, ritual, and the means therefor.

Some forty years after his first reading of the *Śākuntala,* the older Goethe derived the same earlier delight. His later reflections deserve quotation here:

I easily recollect even now the transcendental impressions which this work first created on me. The poet here appears to us in his highest function as the representative of the most natural condition of the most beautiful way of life, of the purest moral effort, of the worthiest majesty, of the most sincere contemplation.[45]

As against this superlative praise we may set a more restrained verdict by an Indian poet-critic, Sri Aurobindo:

A mere poet like Goethe may extend unstinted and superlative praise to *Śākuntala,* but the wiser critical and scholarly mind passes a less favorable verdict.[46]

Kālidāsa's handling of minor characters in *Śākuntala* bears witness to his mature craftsmanship. His genius could present novelty even within the well-defined rules of the Indian dramatic tradition. With conventional writers who blindly follow the rules the minor characters are mere appendages. That is why such plays appear hopelessly unrealistic and artificial. There is a vast gulf between life as actually lived by the people and the one idealized in the plays. Kālidāsa alone manages to present such lifelike characters as the fisherman and the police, the two girlfriends of the heroine in the hermitage and her two hermit-escorts to the palace. Notwithstanding the similarities in heredity and environment, the individuality of each in temperament and personality stands out in Kālidāsa's treatment. The fisherman, for instance, is happy and content in his humble profession. He has a sense of humor in the face of the worst odds. He is at once simple, natural, and forthright. The policemen who catch him are not blind to their immediate self-interest while discharging their professional duty. They delight as much in bullying their prisoner in trouble as in flattering him when rewarded.

Similarly, Priyaṁvadā, true to her name, has only sweet words to speak. She is not only witty and playful but farsighted and resourceful. A foil to her is Anasūyā, with her modesty and outspokenness, her plain sense of duty and unassuming simplicity. Priyaṁvadā can actively promote Śakuntalā's love, but Anasūyā only in an indirect manner.

In their first visit to the city, Śārṅgarava and Śāradvata, the two hermit-escorts of Śakuntalā, are like fish out of water. Śārṅgarava is straightforward in his denunciation of court life and manners and too short-tempered to understand Duṣyanta's predicament. Śāradvata is less effusive, less explosive, less rash, and more understanding.

The character of Kaṇva deserves special mention. He represents the Indian ideal of wisdom wedded to disinterested action. His grief is human, but his detachment is divine. In Sri Aurobindo's words, "the perpetual grace of humanness which is so eminently Kālidāsian, forming the atmosphere of all his plays, seems to deepen with a peculiar beauty in his ascetics."[47] Kaṇva reminds us of sage Vālmīki in the *Rāmāyaṇa* who runs to the aid of Sītā deserted by Rāma.

(d) ESTIMATE. It is impossible to give an adequate idea of the excellences of Kālidāsa's diction ever dear to Indian hearts. His ease and grace, his illuminating imagery and suggestive force, his masterly vocabulary and matchless phrasing are unique in Sanskrit literature. Kālidāsa is essentially a poet, capable of soaring into the region of fancy and going deep into the inmost recesses of the human heart. He achieves his object with an economy of expression and a judicious use of figures of speech, unique in the history of classical Sanskrit literature. He is refreshingly free from the extravagant hyperboles, farfetched imagery, and pomposity of his numerous imitators.

All his plays attempt to probe the eternal mystery that is love, against a vast background ranging from earth to heaven, a love of which sages are sympathetic spectators, angels willing participants, with fate itself ready to lose its sting. Man is raised and purified, not so much by love's delights as by its hardships. This is, in sum, the theme of Kālidāsa's plays which are neither historical nor mythological, but essentially imaginative and poetical. Realism and romance intermingle in different proportions to form the unique amalgam of Kālidāsian fancy.

Judged by modern standards alone, Kālidāsa's limitations are obvious. So would be Shakespeare's. He was as much at the mercy of conventions as any other poet, especially a court poet. The patron had to be humored. Since a play was, in his days, primarily meant for royal amusement, only kings could serve as heroes. Further, the Indian pattern of life and culture imposed its own limitations. The Vedāntic philosophy and religion, insisting on the primacy of the ethical values even in matters of love, compelled Kālidāsa to cast his plots in a set mold. He does not challenge the prevalent world view. What strikes us is his success in revealing human nature and the ideal of human love in the face of such limitations. It is sometimes alleged that Kālidāsa was not alive to the problem of evil. The truth is that evil appears throughout his works in an imaginative form, of which the recurring curse motif is symbolic. Sorrow figures in practically every play, and in the *Śākuntala* we have a masterly analysis of it. Kālidāsa was no blind optimist. He was aware of the place of sorrow in the human lot; yet his faith in the final victory of good made him prefer the pattern of romantic comedy to tragedy. This does not affect the fact that his stories are essentially concerned with sorrow and that, in his world view, joy and sorrow are both inevitable phases of the dynamic life of man.

CHAPTER 3

Men and Gods: The Epics

The ode is bolder, and has greater force
Mounting to heaven in her ambitious flight
Amongst the Gods and heroes takes delight.
—Dryden

KĀLIDĀSA'S claim for the highest place among the classical poets of India is based as much on his poems as on his plays. The age of the natural epic had long passed. He already had before him a set of conventions about *Mahākāvya* or the court-epic. The theme was to be lofty, the style ornate, the meters varied. In cantos ten to twenty the poet was expected to provide minute imaginative descriptions of stock topics like the mountain, the sea, the city, the seasons, battles, weddings, royal sports, sunrise and sunset, besides presenting great kings or gods as heroes. Although inheriting this stereotyped tradition, Kālidāsa, alone in the long history of Sanskrit poetry, could rise well above its limitations and produce two works both of which are, by universal consent, the best two in the genre. These give us an insight into the ideals and aspirations of the Indian people.

Kālidāsa took elements from the *Rāmāyaṇa* and the *Mahābhārata,* from the *Purāṇas* and chronicles,[1] and molded them into a poetic idiom which is still by far the best standard of the Sanskrit poetic sensibility. While the dramatic conventions do impose their restrictions, his genius and imagination can still take wings and fly. Compared with the popular epics of Vālmīki and Vyāsa, Kālidāsa's narrative poems are smaller in bulk but richer in artistic content. Addressed to the elite rather than to the people at large, Kālidāsa's poetic diction is more elegant and refined, if less direct and naïve. The importance of the action diminishes, and its place is taken by descriptions of nature and man in sophisticated conceits. The passions are depicted with an individual touch which reveals at every step the poet's self-conscious art. This is in contrast with the impersonal treatment of elemental and universal emotions that characterizes the earlier epics.

The words, besides their logical value, are enriched with overtones, and the emotion is conveyed by means of verbal cadence and harmony of phrasing. Kālidāsa's personality as a poet is felt not only in the imaginative situations and living characters created by him but also in his style steadily intent on beauty of effect. The poet is seen as a worshiper of beauty, whether in God, man, or nature. If the plays are concerned with the single theme of love, its passionate frenzy and sorrows as well as its purifying power, the poems reveal other dimensions of the imagination, like the historical, patriotic, religious, and spiritual. In terms of Indian criticism, we could characterize the poems as suffused with the sentiments and ideals not only of love, but also of the common good, embracing national, ethical, and spiritual values.

Of the two epics, the *Birth of the War-God* appears to be the earlier in the order of composition. Its first eight cantos are short and compact, knit together by unity of design. The other cantos are ignored here, as their authenticity is for several reasons highly doubtful. Sanskrit critical works, which quote freely from the first eight cantos have no knowledge of these. An uneven style, with no trace of the Kālidāsian imaginative audacity, is an additional pointer to their late composition. Again, these are left uncommented upon by the classical interpreter Mallinātha. The second poem, the *Dynasty of Raghu,* is larger in canvas, more consummate in thought and style, and many-sided in its treatment of the heroes, indicating a more mature mind.

I The Birth of the War-God

Kālidāsa is happy in his choice of the highest conceivable subject for the first of his long poems. Śiva, the supreme god in the Hindu pantheon, is described in the myths as having a consort named Pārvatī who forms, symbolically, half of his person. From one point of view, Śiva is the Absolute who represents the values of Existence, Truth, and Goodness in their immutable state. Pārvatī, or Beauty, stands for the dynamic cosmic activity, whether on the physical or the psychological plane. Śiva, the Good, having the other half for his complement, perforce finds goodness and beauty in everything cosmic, even in what we mortals would see physical evil and ugliness. The cosmic wedding of the two brings forth power as its offspring, destined to extirpate evil symbolized in the demon Tāraka.

In this connection we might note two more explanations of the symbolism underlying the poem, the first by Tagore and the other by Sri Aurobindo:

1. In the commencement of the poem we find that the God Śiva, the Good, had remained for long lost in the self-centred solitude of his asceticism, detached from the world of reality. And then Paradise was lost. . . . How was it regained? When Satī, the Spirit of Reality, through humiliation, suffering and penance, won the heart of Śiva, the Spirit of Goodness, was born the heroism that released Paradise from the demon of Lawlessness.[2]

2. . . . . The central idea of this great unfinished poem, the marriage of Śiva and Pārvatī, typified in its original idea the union of Purusha and Prakṛti, the supreme Soul and dynamic nature by which the world is created; but this type of divine legend was used esoterically to typify also the Nature-soul's search for and attainment of God and something of this conception pierces through the description of Pārvatī's seeking after Śiva.[3]

Even Keith, who is usually restrained in his judgments, admits:

High as Indian opinion ranks the *Meghadūta* which won also the commendation of Goethe, to modern taste the *Kumārasambhava* appeals more deeply by reason of its richer variety, the brilliance of its fancy and the greater warmth of its feeling.[4]

Mount Himālaya, as portrayed by Kālidāsa, is not so much an immense physical mass as a divine personality providing a home for the gods and living a life of his own with Menā for his consort. He is the measuring rod that spans the vast earth from the eastern to the western sea. He is the abode of the choicest gems the earth can offer as also of the most potent herbs. Not all his snowy raiment could detract from his grandeur and beauty. A trivial flaw passes unnoticed amidst an abundance of virtues as is the dark spot of the moon. His cloud-kissing peaks, glowing all crimson with the rocky ocher, color the hovering clouds to produce the fiction of a twilight for the celestial nymphs who hasten for their evening toilet. The rain-bearing clouds hardly reach his mid-height, so that the hermits harassed by rain have only to scale up his sunny peaks to be free. The wild lions and elephants, the gigantic trees, the wind piping through the bamboos, the biting scent of the arboreal sap, the herbs fluorescent by night, the overhanging clouds—all these serve in varied ways for the pleasures of the fairies, wood nymphs, and wild hunters. The lotuses in his exalted lakes are blown open by the sunbeams reaching from below as the sun revolves about his middle. Seeing his opulence and might, the Creator has crowned him the emperor of mountains.

In his human aspect he has Menā for his queen, who bore him a son, Maināka, a winged mountain, and a daughter, Pārvatī. Pārvatī, in her previous life as Satī, Śiva's former wife, had immolated herself in her father's sacrificial fire in protest against the slighting of her husband by her father. The little daughter brought glory as well as graces to her father, even as the light to the lamp, the heavenly Ganges to the Milky Way, and the polished speech to the wise. Though playing with her mates on the golden sands of the Ganges, she could remember all her learning in the previous life.

Kālidāsa's description of Pārvatī's youth is one of the highlights of the poem:

Her features assumed grace and proportion as in a picture by a master artist, or like the lotus unfolding its loveliness at the touch of the rising sun. Her feet surpassed the land lilies in color and softness, and her gait that of the swans. Her limbs were perfect. Neither an elephant's trunk nor a plantain stem could stand comparison with her thighs. The three folds on her midriff were like the steps of Cupid. Her breasts were so shapely and buxom that not a lotus fiber could divide the two. Her arms were softer than the flower *Śirīśa*. One could not tell whether her necklace adorned the neck or her neck adorned the necklace. The moon's beauty does not coexist with the beauty of the lotus. But in Pārvatī's face they blended together.

If at all a flower could be set on a reddish shoot or a pearl embossed in a pink coral, one might get a parallel for the radiant smile about her rubicund lips. Her nectar-sweet voice could turn the cuckoo's notes to jarring sound as from a lute with broken strings. One could not decide whether sparkling beauty of her eyes was borrowed from or loaned to the hinds. The god of love gave up his pride in his lovely bow on seeing her finely drawn eyebrows. The yaks could no longer boast of the excellence of their tails once they looked at Pārvatī's flowing tresses of hair. In a word, she united in herself all the beauty scattered through Nature as if the Creator intended to have a form perfect in all respects.

We have here a typical example of Kālidāsa's unfettered imagination and profound love of nature. Whether in its benign form or fierce aspect, Kālidāsa's poetic soul readily responds to it with an affinity bordering on intimacy. Everywhere he finds nothing but harmony and the manifestation of that beauty which has many mansions. His contemplation of nature is at once sensuous and romantic. His portrayal of feminine beauty in relation to nature becomes the accepted model for all the later poets in Sanskrit.

One day the divine sage Nārada, who happens to see Pārvatī gamboling by her father's side, prophesies that she will win Śiva's hand in marriage. Himavān is so delighted that he does not think of arranging any other match for her. He at once commissions her to wait upon Śiva, who has been practicing penance on the mountain since Satī's tragic self-immolation. Pārvatī, along with two friends, repairs into the presence of Śiva whose purpose for penance no one can tell [Canto I].

The Purāṇic story of the pitiable plight of the gods harassed by the demon Tāraka, and their audience with Brahma the Creator, forms the subject matter of Canto II. Kālidāsa utilizes this occasion to sing a hymn in praise of God Brahma, which contains in essence his own philosophy and religious belief:

You are the Trinity, the One before creation. The three cosmic acts—creation, preservation and destruction—are but phases of you. You sowed in cosmic waters the seed of the universe. In you the first man and woman found their origin. When you are awake there is creation, and when you sleep it is universal destruction. Your day and night mean so many eons here below. You are the uncaused cause. Endless yourself, you end the universe. You without a beginning begin the world; without an overlord, you lord over the universe. You are self-destroyed. You are the liquid and the solid, the gross and the subtle, the light and the heavy, the tangible as well as the intangible—all declaring your protean nature. You are the source of the scriptures, their ritual as well as their fruit. You are both the Nature, ever active, and the Self, her passive witness. You are the first of the Manes, the god of gods, transcending the beyond. You are yourself the eternal holocaust and the priest, the eaten and the eater, the known and the knower, the thought and the thinker.

In Kālidāsa's conception, the godhead represents a perfect synthesis of the Vedic religion and the Vedāntic philosophy, the Purāṇic personal theism with its emphasis on devotion, and the philosophic impersonalism of the Sāṅkhya system. Kālidāsa imaginatively realized the truth—missed by the classical thinkers who developed independently atheistic schools—that God is the link unifying in essence the apparently divergent currents of the pristine wisdom of India. Thus, the *Brāhmaṇas, the Upaniṣads,* the *Bhagavadgītā,* the *Purāṇas* and schools of philosophic thought like *Mīmāṁsā, Vedānta, Sāṅkhya, Yoga, Nyāya,* and *Śaiva* are all harmonized to yield a consistent *Weltanschauung.* Though primarily a poet, Kālidāsa was also deeply read in the Indian classics of philosophy.

Then the story is resumed when the gods relate their harrowing tale of woe at the hands of the demon Tāraka. All their efforts to keep him at bay have been in vain because of his overwhelming strength. Varuṇa, the god of the waters, Yama, the god of death, Kubera, the god of wealth, Sūrya, the sun-god, and the King Indra himself have been routed by him in pitched battles. Viṣṇu's infallible discus, failing to hurt him, has become his necklace. Though their women were raped and their palaces and parks pillaged, the gods have been reduced to helpless spectators. Brahma points out in answer that the demon's might was due to his own boons and that consequently he cannot bring himself to destroy him. One cannot cut down a tree planted by oneself though it should turn out to be poisonous.

At the same time, he assures that their troubles will end if a son is born to Śiva and Pārvatī, since he alone could lead the gods to victory against the mighty demon. The gods confer among themselves as to how they could bring about the desired union. Indra cannot think of anyone better fitted to cope with the task than Kāma, the god of love (Canto II).

We see Kālidāsa at his best in Canto III, where the god of love goes on his errand confidently, tempts the unperturbable Śiva for a trice, but only to be burnt to ashes by the latter's third fiery eye. Here is the master's economy of effort for achieving the maximum of effect.

The canto begins with the speech of Kāma, who boasts of his might in such grandiloquent terms that it acquires ironical significance when we see how he succumbs to the wrath of Śiva so belittled.

The most beautiful part of the canto is the description of spring in Kāma's train. Kālidāsa here makes use of all the poetic conventions with such imagination that they shed their banality. His ever fresh invention imparts life to inanimate objects:

When the Sun like a lover turns toward the North, his new beloved, breaking his pledge to his first love, the South, sighs in sorrow as if in the form of sweeping winds. The Aśoka suddenly puts forth flowery shoots without waiting for the caress of maidens whose feet are decked with jingling anklets. The new mango blossom is the sharp arrow fashioned for Kāma by his general, Spring—the fresh sprouts are its feathers, and the bees are the inscribed letters of Kāma's name. Karṇikāra, so rich in colors, is a flower without fragrance: the Creator is perhaps against heaping all excellences in one.

Curved like the crescent moon in their half-blown state, the pink Palāśa flowers appear like the nail prints left on the beloved sylvan maids in their first amours with Spring. The Tilaka flower decks the forehead of the Spring-lady, the bees form her mascara, the mango sprout her lip and the Dawn her rouge.

The sweet note of the male cuckoo was like a proclamation that Kāma would humble the pride of lovely maidens. When Kāma and his consort Rati arrived with Spring, all couples manifested their love frenzy in action: the male bee drank honey with its mate in the same flower cup; the stag stroked the hind softly with his horn, as she closed her eyes in rapture; the cow elephant offered to her dear mate a lotus-scented spittle from her trunk; the fond cakravāka bird presented his sweet mate a half-tasted lotus bud. The satyr couples were lost in kisses and embraces. Even the trees were hugged fast by their darling creepers with flowers for breasts and red shoots for radiant lips.

But nothing can disturb Śiva's peace, though Nandin on the watch commands silence with his forefinger on his lips. At once the whole forest becomes still, as if it were a forest painted. The trees stop their swaying, the bees their humming, the birds their twitter, and the animals their movement.

Avoiding his sight, Kāma approached the spot where Śiva was lost in meditation. Śiva was poised on a deodar seat covered with a tiger skin. His back erect, shoulders taut and palms outstretched, it seemed as if a lotus had flowered from the center of his lap. His matted locks were entwined with serpents, a double rosary adorned his ears. He was clad in a black buckskin which looked all the blacker by the light of his dark neck. His eyes were focused on the tip of his nose, steady and serene, with controlled breath, like a water-laden cloud without rain, like a vast sheet of water without a wave, like a steady lamp in the windless shelter. Beside the jets of radiance sprung out of his head through its central opening, the light of the crescent moon appeared pale. Thus was he looking inward and absorbed in the Supreme Self.

Kāma shuddered at his sight, but took heart as he saw Pārvatī close by. She was decked in the best flowers of Spring and clad in bright red. The matchless beauty of her limbs was thrown into relief by the dress and the ornaments. It was hard for her to ward off the bee thirsting for her juicy lip. Her arrival was duly announced by Nandin to Śiva, who had just come out of his trance. Pārvatī with her maids greeted him with choice flowers as he blessed her that she might have a devoted husband.

Kāma awaiting his chance, took steady aim and let go his arrow, "Infatuation," at Śiva just as Pārvatī was offering him a rosary of sun-dried lotus seeds. Even valiant Śiva shook just a little, as the ocean might be disturbed by the rising moon. And he turned his eyes toward her face with its ravishing red lips. With her hair standing on end and quivering like a vine putting forth its buds, Pārvatī stood still, lovelier than ever, her looks betraying sweet confusion and her frame arched in suspense.

In the whole range of Sanskrit poetry, this juxtaposition of opposites—the spiritual and the sensuous at their highest together—is unique. Though the conventions of court poetry disfavored such combinations, Kālidāsa struck out a new path in order to suggest his philosophy of life, which reconciles the highest Yoga with the ideal of marriage. The extracts quoted above give an idea of the power of Kālidāsian imagery to lend form to the formless and beauty to everything. The whole of nature strives, as it were, to provide him with the most appropriate and poetic similes. And his dramatic genius is manifest in the way he leads to the climax, Kāma's tragic end.

Soon Śiva, the three-eyed God, regains his composure and notices the archer still in the posture of shooting. He is so enraged that his third fiery eye opens, and Kāma is forthwith burned to ashes. At this, Rati his consort, swoons and Śiva leaves the scene with his hosts. Pārvatī, with all her noble lineage and her own pride of beauty, feels humiliated, and her father bears her away like a white elephant carrying a lotus creeper on his tusk (Canto III).

Rati's lament is the theme of the entire fourth canto which remains unsurpassed as one of the most moving elegies in Sanskrit literature. A poet's vision of life would remain incomplete without his reflections on death. We think of death as an ending. Kālidāsa considers it the beginning of a new existence. We are apt to think in terms of losing, while Kālidāsa stresses what is gained. When we talk of departing, he would emphasize the arriving. Kāma dies in his own body, only to live in countless bodies. The truth, that love is immortal, could not have been conveyed through a better symbol.

On the other hand, grief and bereavement form the very stuff of life, and there is no escaping them. However painful in life, they become sources for some of the "sweetest" poetry our literature knows. Kālidāsa has initiated a new genre of elegiac poetry by the choice of a special meter which, by its softness of tone and repetitive rhythm, accentuates the poignancy of the loss.

How can Rati (lit., "pleasure") survive, widowed of Kāma (the god of beauty and love)? She swoons at the shock and recovers only to weep so bitterly that she makes the whole of nature weep with her:

> Hard-hearted are women indeed, since my woman's heart does not burst though you, the paragon of gallants, are reduced to this pitiable state. Whither could you possibly have fled leaving your mate whose life is bound with yours? Never have you wronged me so far, nor have I ever done you offense. Why do you not now respond to the calls of your beloved wife?

She imagines how all the graces of eager lovers would be labor wasted in the absence of Kāma. Wistfully she reminisces over the sweet moments she spent in his company, but her memories only add to her present anguish. On seeing Kāma's friend, Spring, unhurt, her sorrow is redoubled and she decides to immolate herself at once if only Spring would help her to a pyre. But the mishap is prevented by a divine voice announcing that her husband would be revived at the moment when Śiva should marry Pārvatī (Canto IV).

Pārvatī has by now come to realize the superiority of spirit over matter. She is disenchanted of her personal charms and takes to a life of very rigorous *tapas,* or austerity. What she failed to achieve by her sensuous beauty she is bent on securing through sense control. The efforts of her parents to dissuade her are all in vain. She discards her ornaments to lead the hardest ascetic life. The contrast between her former life of luxury and the present one of dire mortification is pictured in vivid colors. In summer, her person is exposed to fires burning on four sides as well as the blazing sun overhead. In the rainy season, heavy downpours drench her body, and in winter she stands unperturbed in the midst of biting ice. She subsists only on water and moonlight. With this ascetic discipline, her body, though emaciated, takes on a new radiance of spirit.

Śiva can no longer ignore Pārvatī's desire now chastened by *tapas.* He presents himself before her in the disguise of a Vedic student in order to put her to a final test. He starts by pitying her, a shadow of her former ravishing self. Frankly admiring her irresistible native charms, he wonders what the object of her austere *tapas* could be, since it is beyond him to imagine any thing or person unattainable to her for the mere wish.

In minute detail, Kālidāsa depicts the wishes natural to a maiden on the threshold of youth, with maxims and epigrams that have since passed into proverbs. "The gem does not go seeking; it is sought after" is a typical example.

On learning from her maid that Pārvatī is resolved to win the hand of Śiva through *tapas* since her beauty has failed, the student expresses his surprise and regret. He paints Śiva in the most horrid colors and does his best to dissuade her from her ill-advised intent.

How can your hand take Śiva's with cobras hissing all over? How ill-suited your bridal robes would be beside his blood-dripping elephant hide! How ever could your soft, painted soles tread on the rough skeletons of his favorite haunt, the cemetery? How ridiculous for you to ride with him on his old bull! His looks are hideous, his parentage unknown, and his possessions could be inferred from his nudity. Is there in him even a single virtue such as is usually sought in a bridegroom?

The studied eloquence of such passages is the hallmark of Kālidāsa's poetry. Though the characters are divine, the sentiments expressed by them are essentially human and universal.

Pārvatī's resolve is in no way affected by these arguments, and she dismisses him with the observation that the great ones would cease to be great if they could be gauged by dull wits. The Supreme Śiva is at once indigent and a fountainhead of all riches, the lord of all worlds and a resident of the cemetery, terrible in form and grace absolute. When the elements are his limbs, who could say for certain whether he was clad in hides or silks, whether he wore jewels or snakes, whether he was fond of skulls or the crescent moon? At this, Śiva throws off his disguise and reveals himself, reassuring her that he is her slave bought with *tapas*.

Kālidāsa's conception of the godhead is both philosophical and poetic. He never misses the immanent or the transcendent aspects of God. Though his poetry is at first sight mythological and popular, he does not fail to suggest the philosophical foundations of his thought. It is this that makes Kālidāsa stand out as the best spokesman of Indian wisdom, while still remaining a votary of the senses (Canto V).

The poet is no revolutionary. He gladly accepts the traditional world order as well as its social and religious conventions. When describing the preparations for and the celebration of the marriage of Śiva and Pārvatī, Kālidāsa does not miss a single detail of the rites prescribed by his religion for marriages on earth. The sixth and seventh cantos are full of these details which give little scope for the flowers of his fancy. The only noteworthy exception is the vividly realistic picture of the Indian bride presented through Pārvatī. Her guileless innocence and the sweet manifestations of the first flush of love find here a most memorable expression.

The eighth canto is in the nature of an epithalamium. Kālidāsa's fondness for passionate sensual love gets the better of his judgment, as it were, for once. We find Śiva represented as a city gallant expert in all the tricks of erotics slowly overcoming his bride's coy resistance during their honeymoon. Though traditional Indian critics[5] have taken Kālidāsa to task for reducing the supreme gods to human size, they have not forgotten to add that this defect is hardly noticed in the enjoyment of the canto's fine poetry. Here is a random example, describing the moonrise:

> The face of Twilight is being kissed as it were by the rising Moon; the darkness gripped by his rays is like the beloved's braid of hair caressed by fingers, with her lotus eyes closing in ecstasy.[6]

The poem, as we have it from the pen of Kālidāsa, closes with the eighth canto. A later poet, who seems to have felt it to be incomplete, has added nine more cantos to bring the Purāṇic story to its logical conclusion. If the poem ends abruptly with the honeymoon, how can the title, *The Birth of the War-God,* be justified? But the question is not so formidable as it appears at first sight. The central theme of the epic is the marriage itself after the reverse of Kāma's death. The marriage naturally implies the birth of a son, Kumāra, who leads the gods to victory against the demon. The incidents concerned with his birth, growth, and battle are poetically uninteresting, however essential they may be in the original Purāṇic story. The prosaic thought, stilted diction, and moralistic handling of the next nine cantos betray an inferior hand. They need not detain us here.

Sri Aurobindo regards *The Birth of the War-God* as Kālidāsa's crowning work and concludes his stimulating essay on the poet in these memorable words:

> He takes up for treatment one of the supreme fables of the life of the Gods and the Cosmos and in its handling combines sublimity with grace, height of speech with fullness and beautiful harmony of sound, boldness of descriptive line with magnificence of sensuous color in a degree of perfection never before or afterwards surpassed or equalled in poetic literature.[7]

II The Dynasty of Raghu

No poet before or after Kālidāsa could seize the soul of India, the very mind and heart of the Indian people, and articulate the whole nation's ideals and aspirations in immortal verse with such delicacy and perfection as Kālidāsa did. If his genius erected an epic monument to the mythical legends of Himavān in his *Birth of the War-God,* it also embodied the ideals and traditions of its heroic kings in his other epic, *The Dynasty of Raghu.* In the former, he is inspired by legendary lore; the chronicle of great kings gives wings to his imagination in the latter. The first is confined to one theme; it has unity of construction; and there is a single philosophy of life stressed throughout which synthesizes the warring claims of passion and self-control in the ideal union of the Beautiful and the Good. The second is a pageant of supposedly historical royal heroes who actualized the ideals of the land in their own lives, who lived and died for the maintenance of *Dharma.*

The range of the second epic is both vast and varied. There are kings like Dilīpa who adopt an ascetic life to atone for their unwitting dereliction of duty to the gods and are ready to lay down their lives for the sake of virtue. Others, like Raghu, stand for valor and conquest, carrying their victorious arms beyond the borders of India, only to give away their treasures to their needy subjects. We have also kings like Aja to whom love is greater than a kingdom and who die voluntarily in order to join their beloved in heaven. At the center of the whole epic we have the celebrated account of Rāma earlier immortalized by Vālmīki in the *Rāmāyaṇa.* In Kālidāsa's selective treatment, we see, mostly, a saga of the joys and sorrows of family life, the ideals dear to the heart of every Indian, the great trials of life and the worth of moral character.

Nor is the poet unaware of the widening gulf between the great ideals of the hoary past and the drab realities nearer his own time. After Rāma, a host of kings are summarily sketched, each glorious in one way or another, until we come to Agnivarṇa, the last to pay with his life for his passionate excesses. The tragic end of the epic is a prophetic vision, a warning to the nation sliding toward decay. That foppery and libertinism carry their own seeds of destruction is suggested by the abrupt close of the epic on a tragic note.

Recently, it has been pointed out with much convincing argument[8] that Kālidāsa was perfecting in this poem a new genre which was in vogue already among the Buddhists. Buddhist tales were full of didactic accounts of several kings in a royal line, each one representing a different aspect of the ideal meant to be stressed. *Vaṁśa,* or "Dynasty," had almost become a literary form, as illustrated by titles like *Mahāvaṁśa* and *Dīpa-vaṁśa* of the Buddhists, and *Aśmaka-vaṁśa* mentioned by the earliest Indian literary critic, Bhāmaha. What was merely didactic was given a poetic form by Kālidāsa.

Kālidāsa's invention added elements which are found in none of these sources—the *Rāmāyaṇa, the Purāṇas,* and the Buddhist *Vaṁśa*—to make his work national as well as universal. While the Buddhist ideal of asceticism is admitted by him, its excess at the cost of healthy pleasure is deprecated. Kālidāsa's poetry breathes a robust optimism quite unlike the pessimism of the Buddhists. The Hindu ideal of a king as a dedicated slave of his subjects is brought to the fore. Kālidāsa is aware of the dangers of monarchy when it degenerates into despotism, and his whole poem is focused on portraying his kings as putting royal duty above personal considerations.

Again, his art turns away from the mere details of the story to dwell on the beauties of nature or the glory of great characters. His poetry here is elegant with no touch of prose or of artifice, and has drawn unqualified admiration from Sanskrit critics, who fancy that the goddess of poetry herself took the pen from Kālidāsa's hand and wrote his works.

The poem begins with a prayer to Pārvatī and Śiva, wedded to each other like speech and sense. Kālidāsa's prayer is for insight into the right thought expressed by the apt word. He modestly tells us that, like a fool intending to cross the ocean in a little boat, he is undertaking a subject far beyond his powers. He fears that his poetic ambition may turn him into a laughingstock, like a dwarf greedily extending his arms for fruit far beyond his reach. Yet he finds some reassurance in the fact that he is no pioneer in the treatment of the theme. The diamonds have already been cut by his predecessors and he has but to string them together.

We then get a pen picture of the noble features common to all the heroes who trace their descent to the Sun-God himself. They are all pure by birth, ever persevering in the attainment of their objects, lords from sea to sea with their chariots plying between earth and heaven. Duly observing their fire offerings, and fulfilling the wishes of suppliants, the kings mete out just punishment to offenders and never fail in vigilance. They amass wealth only to give away, are reticent in speech for the sake of truth, desire conquest, but only to win fame and raise a family. They study in childhood, seek pleasures in youth, become ascetics in old age, and shed their bodies at the end with the aid of yoga.

Kālidāsa is inspired by these noble qualities of the heroes to try his hand at poetry in spite of his own sense of inadequacy. The first king to attract his imagination is Dilīpa.

Broad-chested, tall and strong, he was the embodiment of the martial spirit; surpassing all rivals in strength, outshining everyone by his dazzling personality, he was outstanding in his sway over the earth. His unique personality was matched only by his wisdom, his wisdom by his culture, and his culture by his action. He was a standing paradox to his subjects, inspiring at once awe and confidence, both invincible and accessible, like the ocean harboring sea monsters as well as gems.

Under his lead the people kept to the path of virtue. He collected taxes from his subjects to enrich them in turn, like the sun drawing moisture from the earth to return it a thousandfold as rain. The powerful army he possessed was but an ornament, as its purpose was served by his own unfailing wisdom and the bow ready in his hand. He kept to himself his state secrets so that his endeavors became known only when they bore fruit. Though unmeasured in knowledge, he was merciful at heart; though unrivaled in liberality, he was untouched by pride.

Dilīpa practiced virtue uncompelled by necessity and pursued the pleasures of life being free from attachment. In him excellence followed excellence, delighting as it were in each other's company. Untempted by the senses, he attained the summit of all knowledge. He espoused righteousness alone with passion. He thus carried a gray head on green shoulders. As he gave universal education, protection, and employment to his subjects, he was their father in fact, their parents siring but their body. He resorted to force only to preserve law and order, and he married only to raise a family. Thus wealth and desire were subordinated to the good in this wise king's scale of values.

With mutual understanding, the king offered sacrifices, and Indra blessed him with timely rains. "Robbery" was but a word in his land, as none saw it practiced. His sense of justice was so perfect that he would admire the good even in an enemy and would exile even a friend who sinned. The Creator seemed to have drawn on all the reserves of his energy in the shaping of such an ideal sovereign.

The ideals of kingship pictured here reflect the highest point that India's culture had reached by the age of Kālidāsa. The poet has presented in brief the very essence of his political philosophy. Though, apparently, he credits Dilīpa alone with these qualities, they belong to all the kings in the poem with the exception of the last. The concept of benevolent monarchy as the ideal form of government finds its ablest exponent in Kālidāsa. On this rests his undisputed claim to be regarded as the national poet of India.

Dilīpa's queen is Sudakṣiṇā, who has been singled out for affection by him out of his large harem. Being without a child, they repair to the hermitage of the *guru* Vasiṣṭha to seek his counsel. As they ride in their chariot they enjoy the beauties of the woodland—the cool, scent-laden breezes, the shrill notes of peacocks, the furtive looks of the deer in flight, the music of the water birds in lovely lotus lakes, and the respectful little presents proffered to them by village folk and forest tribes.

Vasiṣṭha extends to them a warm welcome and discovers that their childless state is the result of a curse of the heavenly cow, Kāmadhenu, who was unwittingly ignored by the king in his hurry to meet the queen on one of his journeys back from Heaven. Only by propitiating her can he hope for a child. However, since the cow is inaccessible, the royal couple are asked to propitiate her by winning the affection of her daughter, Nandinī, living in the hermitage.

The couple address themselves to their appointed task with exemplary devotion. From dawn to dusk they both exert themselves for the welfare of the young cow. Before the king's wish is fulfilled, his mettle is put to a very exacting test by Nandinī. One fine evening, when the king is lost in the beauty of the surrounding mountain scenery, he is suddenly roused by the cry of the cow in the grip of a lion. The king's arm, raised to discharge an arrow, is paralyzed in midair. Strangely enough, the lion starts talking and announces himself as Śiva's agent with magic powers. He is kept, he tells the king, to watch over the deodar tree, a pet of Pārvatī. Anything coming within his reach must be his food.

The king pleads that his duty towards the *guru*'s cow is peremptory. In answer, the lion points out that there is no dereliction involved in failing to do the impossible. When the king, however, persists in his plea, offering himself in place of the cow, the lion ridicules the idea. The king's life is much more precious than a cow's and in saving the life of one cow he would be failing in his duty toward millions of his subjects. The *guru* could be easily appeased by the gift of a thousand better cows. But the king's resolve is firm, and he prefers to die in the fulfillment of his duty to living with a sullied character. At this point the lion vanishes, and the cow expresses her admiration for the king's nobility. As a reward, he is promised a child after his heart.

The whole incident about Dilīpa is only an invention of the poet. It has been devised to present an ideal king who puts moral duty above personal pleasure, who values a fair reputation more than narrow self-interest. We have here one of the best commentaries in Sanskrit poetry on *Dharma,* or moral good. Dereliction of moral duty is the secret cause of all trouble, and strict adherence to it even if it involves penance—is the only means of spiritual progress. This ideal, though utopian, was dear to India's poets, and its best exponent is Kālidāsa.

If Dilīpa represents the value of *Dharma,* his son Raghu after whom the poem is named, embodies the ideal of *Artha,* or worldly good. "Raghu" means all-conqueror, not only of enemies, but of knowledge as well. Under his generalship, the sacrificial horse was so secure that Dilīpa could successfully complete the great horse-sacrifice, though Indra himself was out to prevent its fulfillment. Raghu vanquished Indra in a single combat and won heaven itself for his father.

Apart from this mythical victory of Kālidāsa's invention, we have also a very brilliant account of his semihistorical conquests on earth:

Starting from his capital Ayodhyā, he first marched eastward to the Bay of Bengal, sinking wells in deserts, building bridges across unfordable rivers and clearing forests for human settlement. Thus conquest and colonization went hand in hand. Then he overran the eastern countries as far as the Bay of Bengal. He overthrew the mighty armies of the Suhmas and the Vaṅgas, setting up his pillar of victory on the banks of the Ganges. He crossed the river Kapiśā, humbled the Kaliṅgas, and reached the Mahendra mountain. Being a righteous conqueror, he would not annex the conquered territories to his empire but restored them to their rightful rulers, once they had accepted his suzerainty.

Raghu then proceeded to the south along the east coast and reached the Kāverī River. Thence he marched to the Malaya mountain, defeated the Pāṇḍyas at the mouth of the river Tāmraparṇī, and received precious pearls as tribute. Thereupon he crossed the mountain Malaya, Dardura and Sahya, victorious again over the territory of Aparānta. Then he raised on top of the Trikūṭa mountain a pillar of victory.

Then by a land route he proceeded to the country of the Pārasīkas and in a fierce encounter with the Yavana horsemen he emerged successful. His northerly course took him to the banks of the Sindhu where he routed the Hūṇas. After this he overran the Kamboja country, and across outlying ranges of the Himālayas, he subdued the mountain tribes. Crossing the Lauhitya River, he entered Kāmarūpa and collected tribute from the ruler. Having thus conquered the territories on all sides, the victorious Raghu returned to Ayodhyā and performed the *Viśvajit* sacrifice in which all the conquered kings had to participate.

It has often been argued by historians that we have in Kālidāsa's account of Raghu's conquest a close parallel to the conquest of Samudragupta as described by Hariṣeṇa in his Allahabad pillar inscription, or of Candragupta II, or of Skandagupta.[9] An attempt to read history in a professedly poetic composition like the *Raghuvaṁśa* is, to say the least, unscientific. In fact, there are other scholars who have pointed out with no less cogency that Kālidāsa's account is inspired more plausibly by similar conquests described in earlier works like the *Mahābhārata* and *Kathāsaritsāgara*.[10] What is certain, however, is Kālidāsa's intimate familiarity with every province of the vast Indian peninsula, as he describes the flora, fauna, and social customs of each with exactitude.

Another interesting incident in Raghu's career is the penury he is reduced to after giving away everything during his sacrifice. At this juncture, when the sole wealth of the king consisted of earthen pots, a Brahmin student comes up to him seeking a huge sum of gold needed to pay his *guru*. Little perturbed, the king asks the youth to wait three days in his palace, as he is confident of forcing even Kubera, the god of wealth, to fill his coffers. Well in time, there is a rain of gold in his treasury, showered by Kubera who is afraid of his might. The youth goes away happy, wishing the king the birth of a great son.

Raghu's personality is one of the most vividly drawn in the galaxy of Kālidāsa's heroes. An almost heraldic tone and a tapestry quality are effectively blended with stateliness and grandeur in the poet's eulogy of Raghu. Kālidāsa strikes here, as nowhere else, a personal note of ardent patriotism. He has given a new life to the eulogy, which he found conventional, full of capricious and hyperbolic fancy.

The next king to fascinate Kālidāsa is Raghu's son, Aja. From his boyhood he distinguishes himself as a worthy son of a great father. He shoots to kill an elephant run amuck, only to find a demigod freed from a curse, who favors him with an unfailing missile called the "Swoon-inducer."

Aja is chosen by the poet to symbolize a hero who lives for love and dies for it. The occasion of Princess Indumatī's *svayaṁvara*, or choosing a husband for herself in an open assembly, is utilized by Kālidāsa not only to paint Aja as the most handsome and desirable of all princes but also to present the best features of each province of India. No two suitors are like each other, though all of them possess some excellence or other, to invite the princess's attention. This, incidentally, provides a typical instance of the poet's fondness for traditional Indian institutions like the *svayaṁvara*. His eye for beauty and the lighter side of things is brought out in his characterization of Indumatī:

> As the princess, like a glowing torchlight in the dark, moved on from prince to prince, each face she passed darkened and the one she neared brightened, even like the storied buildings on either side of the royal highway.

To be sure, Aja wins Indumatī's hand but incurs the wrath of the disappointed suitors. On his way to the capital they surprise him with their combined forces, but only to be discomfited by his divine missile. Raghu, awaiting his arrival, hands over to him the reins of the government and retires to the forest to practice meditation. Here again, we see the poet intent on stressing the ideal of combining renunciation with a life of heroic activity.

The recurring theme of fate turning unalloyed joy into tragic misery is strikingly illustrated in Aja. When Aja and Indumatī with their son Daśaratha are sporting with abandon in the lovely park, a wreath of flowers from the sky falls on Indumatī's bosom and kills her on the spot.

Aja's bereavement is portrayed by Kālidāsa in a whole canto with such delicacy of tone and exquisite art that it is one of the highlights of the poem. We get here the poet's reflections on the human predicament, on "death in life and life in death." In depth of feeling and intensity of grief, it is comparable only to Rati's lament in his other poem. This *rasa,* or sentiment of pathos, wrung out of grief itself, is a supreme achievement of Kālidāsa. The eternal mystery of life as well as death is almost unraveled by him in a moment of creative insight, and the truth declared in an almost Buddhistic strain:

> Death is the law of all being,
> And life only an accident!
> If one should breathe even for a moment
> It is so much gain wrung from Death.

This philosophy is put in the mouth of the sage Vasiṣṭha consoling Aja plunged in sorrow. It sustains him only for some time, until his son is old enough to bear the state burden. He then voluntarily lays down his body in the holy Ganges to rejoin his beloved in heaven.

At the same time, Kālidāsa is true to Indian religious belief when he makes the wise Vasiṣṭha explain that Indumatī was only a nymph under a curse, now liberated by death. What appears to the ignorant as a most harrowing tragedy on earth may in fact be no more than the happy beginning of a new life in heaven. Thus Kālidāsa, though primarily a singer of love and beauty, does not ignore the hard fact of death or of sorrow on earth. His creative vision admits tragedy, but goes beyond it by reconciling it with a higher harmony in the divine scheme of things. It is this fact which adds depth as well as breadth to his poetry.

How evil, however slight, inevitably brings on suffering according to the inexorable law of destiny, is the thread that binds all the Kālidāsian heroes into a single pattern. This is true of Daśaratha too, who unwittingly shoots down the only son of a blind sage on a hunting excursion. The divine order is essentially a moral one, and there is no escape for the errant from its grinding operation. King Daśaratha must die of heartbreak at parting from a son, and for the moment the sonless man thinks it is a blessing in disguise. But the pathetic epic story of the *Rāmāyaṇa* runs its full course.

Kālidāsa shows his unerring vision in seizing the essential spirit of Vālmīki's long epic of twenty-four thousand verses and distilling it into a thousand lines of limpid verse. The bare incidents of the birth of the four sons, Rāma, Lakṣmaṇa, Bharata, and Śatrughna, and their education under the sage Viśvāmitra; Rāma's marriage with Sītā; his exploits against the demons; the preparation for Rāma's coronation foiled by Queen Kaikeyī's stubbornness; Daśaratha's death; the exile of Rāma, Lakṣmaṇa, and Sītā; the abduction of Sītā by the demon Rāvaṇa; Rāma's friendship with Sugrīva, the monkey-chief; the slaying of Rāvaṇa by Rāma in battle; and the recovery of Sītā—all this was well known to the people from Vālmīki's epic. Kālidāsa only retells it rapidly with skill, adding new touches of fancy.

But the poet's imagination lingers on the love of Rāma and Sītā which ends in the tragedy of Sītā's banishment. Rāma's memory is stirred as he flies back with Sītā from Laṅkā to Ayodhyā and looks down at the panorama of landscapes, each hill, dale, river, and forest reminding him of their former joys in each other's company. This aerial view of India, described in terms of poetry richly dyed in romance, has won the appreciation of every reader. Yet it is only a foil to the tragedy awaiting Sītā on her return to the capital.

Rāma, the hero of Vālmīki's celebrated epic was the *beau ideal* of Indian kingship. He was looked upon as an *avatāra* of God because of his all-around excellence. Rāma's ideal administration, where no subject suffered from want or fear, imposes on him moral trials of the most exacting nature. When Rāma learns from a spy that his people have misgivings about the decorum of their king choosing to live with a once-abducted queen, he has to face a difficult problem. Rāma knows that Sītā is innocent and chaste, that she deserves nothing but his highest love and regard and cannot be made to suffer for no fault. But a just king cannot ignore the suspicions of his people. In this conflict between two duties, Rāma chooses what he regards as his royal duty, sacrificing what he thinks to be a personal interest. In banishing his queen he invites upon himself the loss of Sītā, who is expecting, and of his future heir. Although this may be an exalted ideal to be set before kings, Kālidāsa's heart flows out in sympathy for the wronged Sītā, and he makes even the sage Vālmīki say that he will never forgive Rāma for his treatment of Sītā.

Kālidāsa appears to have presented the kingly ideal after his heart in his treatment of Dilīpa, Raghu, and Aja rather than of Daśaratha and Rāma. The poet is practically voicing his discontent with Vālmīki's vision by setting up in King Raghu a more magnificent and lovable rival to Vālmīki's Rāma. Viewed in this light, the inner design of Kālidāsa's poem will stand out clear, as also the underlying significance of the poem's title: the most noteworthy among the rulers of the line is Raghu rather than Rāma.

The interest of the poem rises steadily till we come up to Raghu, acquires tragic profundity as we read about Aja, Daśaratha, and Rāma, and flags thereafter in the summary accounts of about twenty-one rulers, with exceptions like the deserted city's wail and the last king's depravity. Kālidāsa's poetic vision is very much affected by the wide gulf between past ideals and the hard actuality as he comes nearer his time. Slowly but surely, he traces the process of the decline and fall of a mighty empire. Kālidāsa's unerring historical imagination invites our attention. The roles of poet and historian were combined in Kālidāsa's time, and Kālidāsa has, in his own way, indicated how the downward trend is due to kings swerving from the great ideals of the past.

The poet touchingly describes the woes of cities deserted as also of kings given to a life of ease and luxury. The last king of the line, Agnivarṇa, is an apology for a hero. He is lost in the pleasures of his harem and utterly unmindful of his duties toward his subjects. He dies of consumption, and the great dynasty of Raghu comes to an end. The note on which the poem concludes is surely indicative of the poet's intention to suggest a lesson to the petty kings of his own time.

CHAPTER 4

Love's Ecstasy and Agony: The Lyrics

WE have seen Kālidāsa exalting both immediate and ultimate life values in his plays and epics. His philosophy is world-affirming without prejudice to the ascetic ideal. His poetry resolves the antinomy between this world and the other, between self-indulgence and self-abnegation, by integrating the best of both in a brilliant synthesis. But in his lyrics we move in a narrower world of pure romance, untouched by care and as if unaware of the Vedāntic goal. While Kālidāsa's place as a world poet is securely based on his plays and epics, it cannot be gainsaid that his two lyrical poems largely account for his wide popularity.

Judged by the number of modern translations alone, the *Meghadūta* (The Cloud-Messenger) perhaps stands first in popularity. The other work, *Ṛtusaṁhāra* (The Cycle of Seasons), though often ignored by scholars owing to its dubious authenticity, still continues to inspire enthusiastic translations in verse.[1] Even those, like Keith, who take it for a genuine work, usually offer the plea that it is a juvenile product, bristling as it does with crudities of thought and diction. For one thing, unlike the other, it has produced no early commentaries in Sanskrit. For another, no book on poetics alludes to it, though referring to every other work of Kālidāsa's. The poem itself contains no clue whatever to its author. Arguments based on parallelisms in thought and expression have not proved conclusive. Here we may note Sri Aurobindo's estimate which finds a uniformity in spirit and treatment underlying all the Kālidāsian works. "A vivid and virile interpretation of sense-life in Nature, a similar interpretation of all elements of human life capable of greatness of beauty, seen under the light of the senses, and expressed in the terms of an aesthetic appreciation—this is the spirit of Kālidāsa's first work as it is of his last."[2]

The ethos and milieu of India favored the rise of a lyric genre perhaps unique in the world. The lyric, in India, is neither a turning loose of the poet's personal emotion, nor an escape from it. It is primarily an exercise of the imagination, which fuses the familiar and the strange, the world within and the world without, into a *tertium quid* that interprets both. The new unity is one of *rasa,* or esthetic pleasure, achieved by means of poetic figures and other devices. So understood, lyricism becomes an essential ingredient of all literature; we find, accordingly, a strong lyric element in Sanskrit classical plays as well as art-epics. The distinction between the lyric and other genres is mainly one of scope and range. The vast canvas of the epic, the exalted theme, the scope for varied *rasas,* or sentiments, is absent in the lyric; but the same intensity is felt in its confined limits. When love is the master sentiment, all that is required for its poetic expression is the presence of the beloved, in the body or in the fancy. Her words and actions are not necessary to kindle the poet's imagination. Anything in nature, animate or inanimate, becomes sufficient stimulus to the poet's feeling. We have lyrics of love-in-union where the beloved is present, and lyrics of love-in-separation if she is not. *The Cycle of Seasons* is a fine example of the first, and *The Cloud Messenger* of the second.

I The Cycle of Seasons

In this short poem of one hundred and forty stanzas, we have neither story nor autobiography. We have only the distilled essence of the pure love of a newly married couple, expressed in terms of the man's overflowing joy. The emotion is a generalized one, and any search for the particular would be unwarranted. According to Indian critical theory, an old recluse might compose such a "love-century" as well as a newly wedded youth. No conclusion about the poet's life from such an imaginative exercise would be justifiable. This attitude should serve as a corrective to much modern criticism of Sanskrit lyrics, Kālidāsa's in particular. The poet's world here is wholly one of illusion, though it be delightful illusion. It should not be mistaken for reality. It is a transcript of appearance, of what *seems,* not of what *is.*

Hence, what are called poetical conventions, to be dismissed as tricks of the poet's trade, will be found to possess a peculiar importance in Sanskrit theory and practice. Simile and metaphor, paradox and hyperbole are seen to be inevitable ingredients of the poetic medium. Thus understood, the unique charm of Sanskrit lyricism can be felt even today. "The truest poetry is the most feigning," says Touchstone in *As You Like It,* and he strikingly describes the Indian attitude. Untruth and half-truth, make-believe and fancy, myth and dream—a strange amalgam of all these constitutes the Sanskrit poet's repertory. That is why the poet was looked upon as a creator, transforming this world of reality into a dreamland of fancy.

Kālidāsa enriched this tradition. To the trite conceits of the professional poet he adds the gleam of his brilliant observation and his subjective vision of nature. That the bird *cātaka* subsists on rain drops gathered directly from the clouds is an old conceit. It is left to the poet to turn it into an example of exclusiveness or of conjugal loyalty. That the god of Love has the choicest flowers for his arrows is a stale fancy; but the beauty of the lotus or the jasmine, the mango blossom, or the lily is what the poet is expected to add. The love life of birds and beasts, creepers and trees, rivers and the sea, clouds and mountains, is something possible only in Sanskrit lyric poetry. Add to it a pulsating life, a minute observation and a fancy charging them with the tender emotion, not to mention the grace and melody of diction, and one gets some idea of Kālidāsa as lyricist.

Before Kālidāsa, the bulk of Sanskrit lyric poetry consisted of single quatrains or a brief sequence of quatrains. There were anthologies in Prākrit of "centuries" on love, as that of Hāla; but there was no sustained and unified poetic piece running to several books, as does *The Cycle of Seasons.* Kālidāsa may rightly be regarded as the founder of this new tradition, which found several imitators in later times.

The poem is divided into six books corresponding to six seasons of the Indian year: Summer, Rains, Autumn, Early Winter, Winter, and Spring. In the tropical climate of India, each season leaves its own indelible impress on vegetation and landscape, and on the life of birds and of beasts as well as of man. The youth who has just awakened to love will find in all nature animate and inanimate, a powerful stimulus or excitant of passion. He is filled with longings for his beloved. It would appear that the perception of beauty in familiar things is a gift of love; and as things change and put on new faces in the shifting seasons of the year, new discoveries are made, by lovers, of the kaleidoscopic variety of nature's beauty. Nature viewed through the glass of passion, takes on, each time, the color of love. The entire earth appears as a woman in love. Indeed, the Indian lyric demands from the modern reader a "willing suspension of disbelief." Like Indian art, Indian poetry too presents not the real, but only "a possible and consistent ideal."

Here are translations of a few selections from each canto:

Summer

The sun is hot, but the moon is pleasant; the clear waters invite to a dip at each sight; delightful are the evenings, and passions are gentle: the summer has set in, my Love! (I. 1)

Sweating all over at each subtle joint, young damsels put away their heavy clothes, and wear light silks about their buxom breasts. (I. 7)

Scorched by the rays of the broiling sun and baked by the burning sand below, the snake lingers with drooping hood in the shade of the peacock's plume—a dangerous guest. (I. 13)

The Rains

The Rainy Season is approaching, my dear, with all the pomp and panoply of a king: his dark clouds are war elephants, his lightnings the royal flags, his thunders the rattling drums. (II. 1)

With plumes outstretched, the lovely peacocks, long love-lorn, have resumed their mad dance with embraces and hot kisses. (II. 6)

Sweet maidens ravish their lovers, with their long hair, decked with fragrant flowers, reaching to their hips, with glitter of pearls on their breasts, their faces flushed with wine. (II. 18)

Autumn

Look! here Autumn comes like a charming bride: clad in a white robe of flossy flowers, with the full-blown lotus for her tinkling anklets; her slender frame lovely with the golden glow of ripening rice. (III. 1)

Like lovely damsels, the streams move slow, with shining girdles of sparkling fish, pearl necklaces of white bird-rows on either bank, and rotund hips of stretching sands. (III. 3)

Like a beautiful maiden's face, the lotus now smiles, caressed by the rays of the morning sun. As the moon goes down, the smile fades from the night lily's face, as of the young wife of a traveler far away. (III. 23)

Early Winter

The cold season is shedding tears of dewdrops on blades of grass, distressed at the weight of lovers on luscious bosoms, his favorite snug resort. (IV. 7)

Winter

This is the season for the warm hearth with the windows shut, for basking in the noonday sun, warm raiment and tender maidens. (V. 2)

Spring

The trees are in flower; the lilies bloom in the lakes. Women turn wanton with love and perfumes are wafted in the breeze. The nights are pleasant, and the days; everything is sweet in May! (VI. 2)

The cuckoo is drunk with mango nectar and kisses his mate with passionate fervor. The buzzing drone on the lotus flower sings a love song in praise of his beloved bee. (VI. 14)

The groves are lit by white jasmines as radiant and ravishing as a coquette's smile. When they tempt even an ascetic's heart, from sense withdrawn, imagine their effect on young hearts filled with fancies of love. (VI. 25)

Though the Sanskrit original is beyond any prose rendering, the specimens given above shall serve as illustrations. The poet is at his best in his treatment of summer and spring. It is more or less a "Lover's Calendar" and dwells on the pleasures of youthful love in ecstatic terms. The nature description is sensuous to a degree, and the passion unabashedly sensual, and perhaps accounts for the neglect of the poem by puritanic pandits and its strong appeal to the young. The poet's style here is sweet and graceful, free from artifice and elaborate effects. The meters are both simple and effective. But we miss altogther the seamy side of life.

In the *Ṛtusaṁhāra,* passion beats and palpitates in almost every line. There is a fresh, open-air spirit about it which is natural and compelling. Kālidāsa employs the ancient Vedic bard's power of incantation, of rhyme, rhythm, and repetition, to bind the human community together in a common emotion. The poem illustrates how a good poem can be composed from the commonplaces of human experience without including any abstruse philosophy.

If we compare this poem with the other works of Kālidāsa, we find that it lacks depth as well as breadth. The complexity of conception, and the vast range of experience evidenced in his art-epics, are certainly missing in this light poem. But it is so because Indian theory pushed the limits of the epic poetry as far as possible, including even science and politics, philosophy and morality, history and legend, religion and art, fact and fiction. The epic form in its original state allowed but a thin streak of the poet's dream and vision. We have seen how Kālidāsa showed his genius in contracting the far-flung limits of the ancient epic and succeeded in evolving the art-epic. The new trend in poetry was favoring artistic excess, word embroidery, shifting moods, and sense indulgence as against the old, which emphasized confidence, courage, religious conviction, and restraint. As Kālidāsa attempted to combine the best of the old and the new, we find a blend of philosophical wisdom and national sentiment, conventional ideas and estheticism, symbolism and straight narration in his art-epics. He took another step and created what was unknown before – a pure lyric.

The importance of the *Ṛtusaṁhāra* in the history of Sanskrit poetry is thus unique. It heralds the dawn of a new romantic movement which gives the primary place to the poet's emotional experience as objectified in artistic language. The new poets might welcome a preoccupation with fashionable society, the music hall, the harlot's house, and the artificial paradise of drink to enrich their experience and touch off their imagination. The place of religious emotion in a former age is taken over by sense delight, and love is the only god that commands universal respect. Kālidāsa's personality was such that he could strike out a middle path, winning the applause of the new as well as the old.

Between the extremes of cloying sensuality of court lyricists who had declared war on the old conventions and the undiluted seriousness of religious and didactic poets of old, Kālidāsa's genius finds for itself a middle way. His plays and epics have a strong lyric element serving the cause of truth and goodness. But in his pure lyrics truth and goodness recede into the background and become handmaids of beauty. This new vision of beauty charges *The Cycle of Seasons* with a new intensity, delicacy, and restraint.

Kālidāsa's estheticism is neither ostentatious nor pretentious as it turns out to be in the works of later Sanskrit lyric poets in the period of decadence. There is an unmistakable tone of equanimity and quiet assurance in his handling of love or nature. That Kālidāsa could conceive of such a poem at all during his time is what deserves praise. For, this poem does not speak of the amours with courtesans after the fashion of his day or sing of the amours with nymphs as in epics. It does not use any convention such as the pastoral, but unassumingly expresses the heartfelt feelings of every leisured Indian of his time, whether in town or countryside.

There is no place in this pure lyric for either betrayed or disillusioned love as in the plays; for there are no problems to solve for the ideal lovers in their honeymoon. There is not even a shadow of pessimism or cynicism or discontent with life. There is nothing except the joy of living, the feeling of radiant vitality. The poet here is quite free in the play of his imagination because in this self-evolved genre, the rules have no application. He is blissfully unfettered by preconceptions and assumptions about poetic themes, poetic materials, and poetic modes. He is not troubled by the changing values in society or the changing fashions at court. That is why Ānandavardhana, the doyen of Indian literary critics, declared that of all forms of poetry, the lyric is the purest and the best. And among all Sanskrit lyrics, *The Cycle of Seasons* remains the first and the last of its kind. No man of taste can read it without coming under its spell.

Kālidāsa obtains the richest effects in this lyric by unobtrusive means, like internal echoes which only a very sensitive ear can discover. It is this, of all things, that wins the admiration of the oldest Indian literary theorist, Daṇḍin. Other masters there are of pun and paradox, alliteration and pleonasm, who work wonders with the compound structure of Sanskrit syntax and who win ready admiration from pandits. But as Daṇḍin points out, the secret soul of poetic beauty lies elsewhere; it lies in the hidden assonance and rhythm that fuse the lines into a whole.

While reading *The Cycle of Seasons,* we catch glimpses of a world of beauty underlying the superficial aspects of existence, and we feel the power of creative imagination which succeeds in establishing contact with that intangible world. There can be no two opinions on Kālidāsa's originality of inspiration, allied to a religious impetus, which is instanced in this lyric with all its deficiencies from a wider point of view. Only in India can one conceive of such a "religion of poetry," which Kālidāsa initiated in *The Cycle of Seasons.* And it is this lyric more than any which is mainly responsible for the numerous legends which the fancy of succeeding generations have woven around his personality. As a modern poet rightly says, "it is not the poet's business to save man's soul, but to make it worth saving."

In Kālidāsa's lyric poem, the regional and national elements meet and imperceptibly mingle, broadening into a universal proportion. If the local atmosphere and coloring, and the love of esthetic, and sometimes exotic, taste, are freely displayed, it comes as a contrast to the excess of the later poets of decadence and wins our heart. In the whole of Sanskrit literature we usually miss the poet's own voice because the poets by and large are scholar-poets: dry, academic, and pedantically accurate to the point of tedium. But *The Cycle of Seasons* is a happy exception. Some basis at least is provided here for the individual voice of the poet himself to break through.

The tendency prevalent among court poets was to hark back to the traditions of the past rather than dwell upon the realities of the present. This meant stilted language and outworn ideas. But in Kālidāsa's lyric we see for the first time the

Sanskrit language in all its freshness and vigor. His word pictures have a keen edge and sharp outline. Every quatrain in this lyric shows that Kālidāsa is not simulating a correct poetic emotion like his later imitators, but writing from his own experience.

II The Cloud-Messenger

At youth's coronation, Kālidāsa, you took your seat,
Your beloved by your side, in Love's primeval paradise;
Earth spread its emerald-green carpet beneath your feet,
The sky held over your heads its gold-embroidered canopy.
—Rabindranath Tagore[3]

And Meghadūta, the cloud-messenger,
Who ever seeks him not as a friend of the soul?
—Goethe[4]

The Meghadūta is without a rival in the whole elegiac literature of Europe.
—Fauche[5]

These eulogies may serve as an index of the perfection attained by Kālidāsa in the present poem. Breaking down national barriers, it has won unstinted praise from poets and critics alike. Some in the West have called it an elegy, some a monody, and others a lyric. But all are agreed that it is a perfect gem of its kind. Among Indian commentators, too, opinion is divided whether it is to be classed as a long poem or a short epic. Sthiradeva, an ancient commentator in Sanskrit, is alone in calling it a "toy-epic" (*krīḍākāvya*). He takes pains to illustrate the chief epic features to be found in it, with love-in-separation as the dominant tone. The celebrated commentator Mallinātha is said to have observed that the appeal of the cloud-poem grew with his advancing years.

It is not easy to pigeonhole this imaginative piece in the confines of any genre. It is *sui generis* and marks the appearance of a new genre. The single character that appears in it is a *Yakṣa,* or demigod. But he has no heroic action to his credit. The entire poem is his reverie, induced by the sight of the first rain cloud. If he cannot be thus fitted into the definition of the epic hero, the only other character entitled to be so regarded is the personified cloud. But the latter, being inanimate, refuses to be so classed. All its actions, movements and feelings are sheer products of the poetic fancy. The device of turning an irrational being, a parrot or a swan, into a messenger of love is not unknown to the Indian romantic tales or epic episodes like Nala's in the *Mahābhārata*. But it is to Kālidāsa's credit that he initiated the ingenious experiment of making a whole poem out of this idea. Thanks to his imagination, the inanimate cloud is instinct with life and becomes the ideal messenger between a love-lorn couple.

When the poem opens, the demigod has lost his divine powers because of his lord's curse and is an exile in the hills of central India. He is introduced to us as an officer of state under Kubera, the Lord of Wealth, in his celestial city Alakā, situated on a towering peak of the Himālayas. According to the myths inherited by Kālidāsa, the *Yakṣas* are that class of demigods who are wholly and solely dedicated to the pursuit of sensual pleasures. The curse, involving as it does his separation from his beloved for a year, is, therefore, the direst punishment conceivable.

The motif of the curse is, as we have already seen, a recurrent one in Kālidāsa, in his plays as well as epics. It points to an essentially moral cosmic order, one which could not be transgressed without inviting upon oneself the visitation of suffering. Joy and suffering are thus explained in terms of *karma*, or human action which has moral implications. Not even demigods are exempt from its inexorable decree. In the Indian conception, sensual indulgence is no sin when it is well within the limits of morality; but when it sets at naught the demands of moral duty, it sets the wheel of retributive destiny in motion; and suffering, often out of all proportion to the lapse, is the result. But suffering, however, excruciating, is only a passing phase and is not unrelieved by hope. In this view of life, tragedy loses its sting, though pathos receives its full measure.

The *Yakṣa* of the Cloud-Messenger, then, typifies the lover plunged in sorrow owing to separation from his beloved. Every object of beauty in nature fills him with longing and gives an edge to his distress. The same vines and flowers, lakes and fish, the moon and the breeze, the clouds and the rivers that once fostered his love, now become so many instruments of killing agony in the absence of the beloved. True love, which is to be distinguished from mere lust, thus gains in depth without losing its fervor. The frenzy of enjoyed love is at once impetuous and fleeting; it cloys. But with its dross burned out in the furnace of sorrow, it becomes a precious and noble emotion. Sweet is love, but sweeter the memory of love. What is lost in fact is made up by fancy playing round reminiscences of the past and future visions. Kālidāsa realized that this "sorrowing love" was a fitter theme for immortal verse than love lost in rapture, and he wrote a whole poem to prove it.

The unity of the poem is thus one of mood, not of incident or character. Although the mood has been characterized as romantic or idyllic or elegiac, the fact is that it is essentially lyrical. Though the treatment is reminiscent of the literary epic or ode, it has its individuality in the monotone of the chosen meter as well as its choral quality. The beauty of the poem depends almost entirely on the thoughts and images that arise from a contemplation of the immediate natural landscape, and on the flights of fancy that spring out of a love-filled heart.

The poem is in two parts, the first given to a description of the Cloud's route from Rāmagiri to Alakā, the second meant to portray *Yakṣa*'s pining wife to whom is directed the reassuring message sent by him through the Cloud. In the first part, all the beauty of the Indian landscape in the rainy season, varying from region to region, unrolls itself before the mind's eye of the poet. How much the poet loves his land, its every bush and fern, bird and insect; how his heart leaps up to behold a rainbow across the dark cloud, how he cherishes every sacred temple and river; how much he admires the city as well as the countryside; how ravished he is by feminine charm—all this reflects itself in verse after verse.

Once the autobiographical nature of the first part is admitted, it is not difficult to see the same instanced in the second part too. Scholars have argued that Kālidāsa must have been an ambassador subject to long absences from home.[6] Attempts are made to trace exact correspondences between the palaces described in the poem and epigraphical records in the different localities. But Indian criticism tends to hold that a poem is by definition imaginative and to read realistic details of personal life is unwarranted.

We have several recensions of the poem because of its wide popularity; the shortest consists of only one hundred and eleven verses,[7] and the longest of one hundred and twenty-seven—all in a single meter, each quatrain consisting of seventeen syllables. We have more than twenty commentaries in Sanskrit alone. Kālidāsa's use of imagery is so striking here that many of the verses are found freely quoted in works on Sanskrit poetics.

Let us now turn to a detailed survey of the poem itself. The *Yakṣa,* fallen out of his master's grace, is living the life of an exile in a lone hut on Rāmagiri, hallowed by associations of Rāma and Sītā in Vālmīki's epic. The hut is set in the thick shade of forest trees, with clear waters running nearby. Four months have passed out of the twelve-month, when a cloud lingering on the hilltop catches the *Yakṣa's* eye. It is like an elephant at play.

The sight makes the *Yakṣa's* heart heavy and languid. His thoughts turn to his beloved far away and he can hardly check his tears:

Even a happy man's heart is ruffled at the sight of a cloud; so what need be said of one whose beloved is so far away?

He fears the advent of the rainy season for his wife's sake more than for his own; fears her tender heart might break if he does not send her a reassuring message in time. He gathers the best flowers on the hill and greets the Cloud with them as a friend in need:

Is not a cloud a dull mass of smoke and light, water and wind? And should not a messenger have an alert body and mind? Such thoughts did not strike the *Yakṣa* at all. He stood there suppliant. Verily, the love-lorn cannot tell the inanimate from the animate!

He praises the Cloud's high birth and noble office; its kindly nature and generous heart. He describes his own pitiful state and prays for sympathy. The good turn to be done is but simple: his consoling message is to be delivered to his pining wife at Alakā.

Alakā is the City Beautiful whose high mansions are bathed in the eternal soft light of the crescent moon crowning the crest of Śiva who dwells in the city's outer park.

This illustrates Kālidāsa's suggestive power for which he is a byword in Sanskrit criticism. The abode of all love and luxury, the utopian city of Alakā—there is no such name in the actual geography of India—is ever presided over by Lord Śiva, the good. The denizens of the city are immersed in the enjoyment of love as well as of the arts, like music, dance, poetry, and painting; but their sensuality is held in check by the presiding influence of the Almighty who is all-good. These overtones of associated meanings, which form the very essence of Sanskrit literary appreciation, are missed in translation.

By accepting the mission, the Cloud will be helping not only one man, but the vast number of travelers away from home. He would be earning the gratitude of all their wives, since no unfettered man would venture to be away from his wife in the face of the Cloud's bidding.

Softly, and ever so gently, will the wind push you on! The delighted songbird to your left honors you with his song. The white cranes will attend on you in rows, thanking you for the gift of progeny.

The personified Cloud is throughout pictured with all the traits of a universal friend. The *Yakṣa* assures it that it will surely meet the faithful wife anxiously counting the days. For,

during separation, hope is the stalk which usually holds the flower-like heart of women from suddenly going to pieces.

The company of red-beaked white swans with lotus stalks in their beaks is an added attraction to the Cloud, as they would be accompanying him as far as the Mānasa lake on Mount Kailāsa, that is, almost up to his destination. So the Cloud is called upon to bid farewell to its eminent friend, Mount Rāmagiri, yet bearing Rāma's footprints:

Every time the Mount meets you, there are warm tears of joy in his eyes betokening the bond of friendship.

Next, the route to be taken by the Cloud is described. There are mountaintops enough on the way to provide comforting rest if the Cloud should feel weary. And there are streams too to add nourishment to its body exhausted by raining:

You will be greeted by the startled looks of guileless ascetic-girls when they mistake you for a peak of the mountain blown away by the wind as you set out on your northerly course. But remember not to rub against the mighty trunks of Space-Elephants!

The Sanskrit word *Diṅnāga* alludes to the mythical elephants in space said to bear the weight of the sky in all the eight directions. But two late commentators see also a veiled hint to Diṅnāga, a great Buddhist logician (c. A.D. 400). Since punning is not in Kālidāsa's vein and we have no confirmation of the story from any other source, this cannot be taken to prove the chronology or biography of Kālidāsa.

The *Yakṣa* resumes his narration:

Oh, what a wonderful rainbow it is which starts at the tip of yonder anthill right in front of you! Your lovely self looks lovelier still, like Lord Krishna's in the cowherd's garb with the flashing sheen of a peacock plume. The country lasses drink you up with their warm looks: they know not the art of twitching their eyebrows, but know that you are the harbinger of harvest.

Crossing the plateau of Māla, the Cloud can reach Mount Āmrakūṭa. For the good turn of putting out the forest fires, the Cloud can be sure of a welcome from the grateful mountain:

As you, black and glossy as a maiden's plait, rest on the mountain peak, its sides all yellow with ripe wild mangoes, the divine couples moving in the sky will enjoy the sight as if they saw Earth's broad breast, white all round and tipped with black.

This is one of the samples of Kālidāsian fancy, which abounds in the poem. We have equally fine descriptions of bushes reminding one of the trysts of tribeswomen, the river Narmadā with its stream shattered to bits by the giant rocks at the foot of the Vindhyas, like "a streaked tracery on the back of an elephant," the water itself colored and flavored by the fallen jamboo fruits, like medicine to cure the Cloud of his fits of sickness.

The track of the passing cloud is traced by stags as they see the golden-brown buds of the palms and the first flowers of wild plantains, and smell the sweet scent of the rain-soaked earth in burned forests. Every mountain will thus beckon the cloud to stay. The peacocks will give him a welcome of song and dance with unfolded plumes. But, for the *Yakṣa's* sake he must not tarry.

He will soon reach Daśārṇa, where the garden hedges will be white with thorny shrub, the holy fig trees bustling with nest-building crows, and the jamboo groves black with ripe fruit.

Its celebrated capital is Vidiśā. There you shall win straightaway the delights of love. For you can drink the moisture of the Vetravatī as her waves dance, as a lover taking his beloved's frowning face with a kiss.

Some modern critics have used the term nature-eroticism to bring out the unique Kālidāsian quality in such fancies. Nature is not merely animate in Kālidāsa; it is, but only at times, downright erotic. Oftener, as we shall presently see, we find nature breathing a spirit of holiness and spirituality.

The hill Nīcais is the Cloud's next halt. The mount is thrilled as it were with its palms in full bloom. Every natural cave in it still reeks of the city courtesans who have used them for their rendezvous with their lovers. The Cloud will move on, watering the jasmine vines on the banks of rills, and looking down on the beauty of flower girls whose lilies, worn on the ears, fade as they wipe off the sweat from their cheeks.

The *Yakṣa* makes a special plea for including the lovely city of Ujjain in his itinerary though it does not lie right on his way to Alakā. He adds that the Cloud would lose the cynosure of all eyes should he miss the lovely tremulous looks of city belles startled by his lambent lightning.

On his way to Ujjain is the river Nirvindhyā, passionately awaiting his arrival and revealing her charms invitingly. The birds, frightened by the peals of thunder, splash the ripples, reminding one of the jingling girdle, her halting current laying bare the eddy like a navel unveiled. Her slender current is the plait of hair, and her body looks pale from the sere leaves fallen from trees lining the banks.

In the conventional and ready-made imagery inherited by Kālidāsa, the rivers were the consorts of the Sea; he makes them the love-lorn wives of the Cloud. The symbolism of their mutual dependence is transparent.

Then comes the kingdom of Avantī, where every village elder is well versed in the romantic tale of King Udayana. The Ujjayinī city (modern Ujjain), a veritable fragment of the choicest heaven on earth, is its capital; and its residents are most fortunate indeed, as

the morning wind across the Siprā river, swelling the music of the cranes and wafting the scent of fresh-blown lotuses, washes, like a fond lover, the weariness of ladies after the night's revelry.

The scented fume used by women to dry their hair in every home escapes through the latticed windows to fatten his body. The pet peacock will pay him the homage of dance. And the Cloud can rest for the night on the terraces, scented by flowers and bearing the red imprints of the lac-painted soles of the belles.

The city offers not only esthetic delight but also religious merit. The very hosts of Lord Śiva will admire the Cloud as his color reminds them of the Lord's throat. The temple groves sway in the scented breeze across the Gandhavatī, thick with lotus pollen as well as the cosmetics of beauties bathing in its waters. Whatever the time of the Cloud's visit to the Temple of Mahākāla (another name of Śiva), he should wait till sunset to participate in the evening worship. The Cloud's deep rumblings may well become the drumbeats in the temple's concert of dance music. The dancing girls, with jingling girdle bells, wave the jewel-set chowries till their hands ache. Oh, how they would thank with sidelong glances the cloud for its healing showers on their love-bruised bodies:

> That is the time when Śiva begins his dance, with his arms stretched out like mighty branches of a tree. O Cloud, you can clasp them all in your expansive form and glow like a crimson hibiscus flower in the twilight of the setting sun. Śiva Himself shall take you for his garment of elephant hide dripping with fresh blood, and Pārvatī, her first fright overcome, will bear witness to your devotion.

Eroticism here suddenly gets transfigured into religious devotion. To connoisseurs of Indian art and sculpture, the figure of the dancing Śiva as Naṭarāja, or King of Dancers, is not unknown. The Lord's dance is a symbol of the cosmic rhythm. The highest worship is in self-effacement, which results in self-fulfillment. The cloud is pictured here as the ideal devotee. Kālidāsa has captured the underlying truth of all Indian religion and art in one glorious image. There is no enmity between the supreme delight and the lower delights. Sensual delight, esthetic delight, and spiritual delight do not exclude but involve each other. Kālidāsa singularly stands out as an exponent of this synthetic Indian culture.

The cloud can help the women of Ujjayinī as they go to their trysts under cover of night by flashing his lightnings instead of frightening them with his peals of thunder. If his lady, the lightning, should weary, he should rest with her on the high stories of mansions where doves go to sleep. At dawn, however, he should resume his journey without blocking the rays of the rising sun,

For his rays have to awaken the straying lovers so that they return to their true loves and wipe their night's tears. Even the sun has to wipe the dew tears from the waterlily's face.

Gambhirā is the next river awaiting the Cloud's amorous attention. In her limpid waters his shadow will find a ready entrance as in a pure heart. The white waterlily and the black fish are the white and black of her sparkling eyes. Her whole body is bared to him; her blue water-robe is tucked lightly in her reed-hand to show the sandy groin.

Further on, a cool breeze shall lead the Cloud to Mount Devagiri where the temple of Lord Skanda (son of Śiva) stands. Here the Cloud may change to a flower-like form, to bathe the god with flowery rain in worship. Skanda is, indeed, the light greater than the sun, begotten by Śiva to protect Indra's army! Pārvatī is so fond of him that she fondly adorns her ear with a plume fallen from Skanda's peacock! The Cloud can make that peacock dance by his rumbles and win the god's favor.

Then the flowing river Carmaṇvatī invites the Cloud's caress. When the dark Cloud bends over the river, it will present a sublime sight to the gods moving on high, who think it is Earth's pearl necklace, the stream itself the pearl string, and the Cloud its sapphire pendant.

Beyond the river lies the city of Daśapura and, passing it, one comes upon the Kurukṣetra, where the epic battle (of the *Mahābhārata*) was fought. The river Sarasvatī, hallowed by legend, flows nearby. Her sweet waters had once cured Balarāma of his thirst for wine. No wonder the Cloud's heart would be sanctified by her touch.

Then Kanakhala, where the sacred Gaṅgā descends to the plains! The Cloud may follow her to the source, ascending higher and higher, as on a staircase, to heaven itself. Gaṅgā's white foam is like her triumphant laughter at the discomfiture of Pārvatī in the contest for Śiva's hand. She holds down Śiva Himself by the hair with her ripple-hand. If the Cloud should stop to drink her crystal waters, there would be again the beauty of the stream's confluence with the Yamunā.

Mount "Snow-White" should be in sight by now. The dark cloud on its peak will look lovely, like the dark mud kicked up in play by Śiva's white bull. The yaks may have their tails singed by forest fires raging over the pines, but the Cloud can end their pain by putting out the fires. In fact,

> The wealth of the good is meant for the redress of the needy!

Unicorns might try their strength against the Cloud, but only to be worsted.

When Lord Śiva's holy footprint comes into view, the Cloud has to stop and go round it in prayer. The gods worship it always, and devotees are cleared of sin and gain deathless heaven at sight of it:

> The wind is playing the flute through the bamboos; nymphs are chanting the glory of Śiva; and if you should beat the drum through your rumbles resounding in the caves, the orchestra for Śiva's worship would be complete.

Proceeding further north through the "Swan's Pass," the Cloud will reach the towering Kailāsa peak. Such a huge mass of whiteness it is that one takes it for the laughter of Śiva himself. In the precincts of Kailāsa, Pārvatī might be seen walking hand in hand with Śiva. It is the time for the Cloud freezing into ice and providing a solid foothold for them. What greater bliss can there be for a devotee than the touch of the feet of the Supreme! The delights in store for him there are manifold: the nymphs at play, that would convert him into a shower-bath chamber; the golden lotuses in Lake Mānasa; the white elephant of Indra sporting about; the celestial wish-yielding tree itself:

> There lies Alakā city on the lap of Kailāsa as on a lover's lap, with her Gaṅgā-girdle loosed. She will place you on her high-storied head, even as a belle mounting the pearl ornament on her curly hair!

This is a detailed analysis of the first book of the poem, which is sweet, sensuous, and passionate. The unique atmosphere of the Cloud-Messenger is fashioned of elements typically Indian.

To all intents and purposes, this part of the poem is a description of hills, rivers, mountains, forests, cities, temples, and, incidentally, women. We have no catalogue of drab geographical names in Kālidāsa's poem. All nature pulsates with life. The Cloud is the lucky husband of many river-wives, each singularly charming. The mountains are his intimate friends whose hospitality he enjoys at every halt. All the cities have a double attraction: the sacred temples on the one hand, and the lovely ladies on the other. The poet's fine sense of color and sound, smell and taste, is illustrated in every image. What is more, all this sensuality is chastened and sanctified by the fervor of religious devotion. To the Indian poet, the pleasures of life are welcome when enjoyed as a gift of the Almighty. Beauty itself is God's creation, and its enjoyment the privilege of enlightened man, whether it be in nature or in man. This practical *Weltanschauung* of the poet, though evident in all his works, finds its best and frankest expression here.

Kālidāsa is reputed to be a master of suggestion, meaning more than he states. In *The Cloud-Messenger* he also states what he suggests. General maxims are strewn all through the poem, which are valued high in Indian rhetoric. They have become the common possession of the elite of India.

If the first part of the poem is thus a kind of a nature ode, the second part is an idealized or utopian lyric of enduring love. The central personality here is the lovesick wife of the *Yakṣa* in the dream-city of Alakā. First, the poet paints a vivid picture of the allurements of this fairyland whose immortal denizens carouse and revel in love. Against this background, the personality of the pining wife is portrayed in pathetic colors. How time hangs heavy upon her, and how she is overcome by sorrow despite her numerous attempts at diversion, is the main theme exercising the poet's fertile imagination. The poem closes with *Yakṣa's* message, after which it is named. Only a brief summary is furnished below:

The mansions of Alakā are vying with the Cloud, as it were: the graceful women are lightnings, the wall paintings so many rainbows, the concert drums the rumblings, the crystal pavements the inner moisture, and the turrets raised aloft rival its height. All the flowers of all the seasons set off the beauty of the ladies here. With their fair consorts, the *Yakṣas* resort to the crystal-paved terraces to drink the choicest wines and make love while the drums are beating softly. Oozing moonstones relieve the languor of women after their night of passion. Clouds escape through windows like thieves when they spoil, by their moisture, the lovely paintings on the mansion walls. Ashamed of being disrobed by their lovers, the maidens try in vain to put out the lamplight of jewels by sprinkling them with saffron dust. The nocturnal escapades of the wantons are betrayed at sunrise by flowers that have slipped from their braids and ears, or by scattered pearls from their torn necklaces. Afraid of Śiva's presence, Cupid will not shoot his flower-arrows; but his object is gained by the unfailing wiles of the women themselves.

The *Yakṣa*'s dwelling is over there, to the north of Kubera's palace, with its archway discernible from a distance like a rainbow. The lovely coral tree, bowed down with blossoms at the gate, will serve as a landmark. Not far is the lake built with emerald steps, wherein golden lotuses blow with beryl stalks. The swans dwelling in it care not to move to the Mānasa lake, though so close, even after seeing the Cloud. On its bank stands the pleasure hill, covered with golden plantain groves, its summit set in sapphire. The red Aśoka tree and the saffron are there, beside the bower bounded by amaranths. All these share the affection of the lady of the house. Right in the middle is the golden peacock perch, crystal-pedestaled and inlaid with green gems. Every evening the lady gives lessons in dancing to her pet peacock, with claps that make her bracelets tinkle. Finally, on the door itself are painted the holy conch and lotus. These signs would help the Cloud locate the place in spite of changes that time has made.

Resting for a while on the pleasure hill, the Cloud should peep in, with a mild flash of his lightning eye, to catch a glimpse of the lady:

> She, who is slim and young, with pearly teeth and red lips, with slender waist and glances like a frightened fawn's, with a low navel, heavy hips, and a form slightly bent by the weight of her breasts—she, in the world of young damsels, would appear as the masterpiece of the Creator's art.

She is the *Yakṣa*'s wife, his very life, spare of words but rich in beauty. In his absence she would be pining like a lotus blighted by frost. With tearful eyes all swollen, lips faded by hot sighs, her hair loosely hanging, her face resting over her hand, she will be lackluster like the moon hidden by clouds. She might be offering worship to the gods, or painting the *Yakṣa*'s portrait, or talking of him to her pet parrot. Or she might compose a song about him and play it out on her lute. But she would break off in the middle, forgetting the tune or the song. Or she might be counting, with flowers placed in worship at the doorstep, the days of separation yet to go. Or she might be lost in a wishful dream,

For such indeed are the diversions of women when they are separated from their lovers.

While the days are thus somehow spent, the nights will prove harrowing. Sleeplessly rolling on the bare ground, she calls for compassion:

Languishing with agony and reclining on one side of the hard bed, like the moon with a single digit on the eastern horizon, she would pass, with hot tears, the lonely long-drawn nights—nights that once would slip away in my company.

She would desire sleep only to dream of union. Her hair, now unkempt and worn in a single braid, bears witness to her devotion to the *Yakṣa*. The moonlight, which once delighted her, now fills her with anguish. Her pale, unadorned body or her slovenly dress would move the Cloud to tears. For the softhearted are by nature moved to pity.

As soon as she sights the Cloud, her eyes are sure to throb "like the blue waterlily shaken by sporting fish." Her thigh will shudder with expectation. By chance, if she should be asleep when the Cloud arrives, he had better not disturb her rare dream-union but let her to be awakened slowly by the cool morning wind. Then, catching her eye with his lightning flash, the Cloud should talk to her gently from the window:

Cloud am I, a dear friend of your husband who lives still; I am here, bearing in my bosom the treasure of his message to you. You know that my nature is to quicken by my gentle thunder every traveler tiring on his way to hasten and caress his pining wife.

At this she will take heart and turn to you, as Sītā of yore welcomed Hanumān with breathless expectation. She will then be all attention. For woman, tidings of her husband borne by a friend bring joy that is but short of union.

He inquires after your welfare from his retreat at Rāmagiri. Denied free movement by cruel Fate, in fancy he unites his body with yours, both equally slimmed and fevered; his eyes with yours tear-bedimmed from anguish; and his sighs with yours steaming hot in grief. He who would once rather whisper in your ears the most unsecret things for the mere joy of your touch, now, being out of earshot and sight, is constrained to send a message to you from afar.

Now for the message itself:

I try to see your form in the tender creepers, your glance in the eyes of the timid deer, the comeliness of your face in the moon, your glossy hair locks in the rich plumage of the peacock, and the grace of your eyebrows in the little ripples on the river. But alas, my love, in no one thing is your likeness to be had in full.

With crude pigment I try to paint on stone your figure in a pose of feigned anger with myself down at your feet. But my vision is blurred by tears again and again, and the picture remains unfinished —cruel Fate will not brook our union even in a picture!

The sylvan goddesses themselves are moved to tears at the sight of my empty arms hugging you in dream. The southbound winds from the Snow Mountain, bearing the pungent scent of new-burst deodar shoots, are fondly greeted by me with open arms in the belief that they may perchance have brushed your limbs.

Would that the long night had shrunk down to a moment! Would that the shimmering noontide were subdued to morning sunshine! Such are the fancies I indulge in, desperate that I am.

With fond hopes of the future I manage to cling on to life. You too, O love, must not give in to excessive anxiety. Who on earth can ever have either joy or sorrow unmixed? Like the spokes of a revolving wheel, the turns of life have their ups and downs.

My curse shall end in four months. Resign yourself to what cannot be helped. Time will come when we shall have our heart's content on moonlit nights.

You know the night when you suddenly woke up from sleep to sob aloud, and I had to coax you insistently for an answer—"Oh you rogue, I dreamed you were making love to another!"

This incident, known only to us, ought to show that the message is genuine. They say love declines in separation. But the truth is that love fostered by fancy is the stronger for being denied its due.

The message entrusted, the *Yakṣa* hopes the Cloud will not turn down his request. He takes its silence for acceptance. Does not the Cloud feed the thirsty birds without a word spoken? The poem concludes with a wish that the Cloud, as a reward for its good turn, may never have to part from its beloved lightning.

In the Sanskrit original, the poem is enthralling. The green paradise of innocent love and beauty, the songs and kisses, the flowers, the lutes thrumming and the drums sounding, the wine flowing in moonlit halls, the woods and the nymphs—these call to mind the classical Arcadia, and the pastoral Sicily of Theocritus. With one important difference: the pangs and griefs of loyal love and its finest delights are equally bathed in the subdued light of the spiritual, which is never allowed to remain long out of sight. Unlike ancient Rome, India found a unique synthesis of the divergent claims of hedonistic passion and religious devotion, rank sensuality and ascetic renunciation, estheticism and philosophic calm. No wonder Kālidāsa so endeared himself to the hearts of Indian lovers of poetry.

Kālidāsa's admirers in India have paid homage to his genius by attempting imitations of this new genre. As early as the eighth century A.D., the Jain polymath Jinasena thought it worthy enough of a tour de force weaving every line of *The Cloud-Messenger* into a new quatrain to yield a eulogy of the prophet Pārśva. But no imitation could match Kālidāsa's art.

CHAPTER 5

Kālidāsa: A Summing-Up

I *Western Views*

IN the course of our analysis and estimate of Kālidāsa's works the chief merits of the poet have been broadly touched upon. The critical judgments of widely different scholars, past and present, are in general agreement about his greatness.

Herder, the celebrated German poet, as quoted by Max Müller,[1] observes: "Do you not wish with me that, instead of these endless religious books of the Vedas, Upavedas, and Upāṅgas, they would give us the more useful and agreeable works of the Indians and especially their best poetry of every kind? It is here the mind and character of a nation is best brought to life before us, and I gladly admit that I have received a truer and more real notion of the manner of thinking among the ancient Indians from this one Sakuntala, than from all their Upnekats and Bagvedam."

Reviewing Sanskrit poetry in general for the *Quarterly Review* of 1831,[2] Dean Milman admits that, "however encumbered with monstrous and extravagant fiction, and a wild and incoherent mythology, it not only excites our interest, but even to European ears may be found to abound in passages rarely perhaps of striking grandeur or energy, but often of the most exquisite delicacy, of the softest tenderness, of infinite variety and gracefulness of fancy, and what may not least surprise our readers, of the purest simplicity." This was at a time when Oriental poetry was proscribed in the mass as offering little more than a confusion of florid diction, and turgid and fantastic poetic conceits.

But soon, Monier Williams could say of the *Śākuntala*: "It combines the majesty of Homer with the tenderness of Vergil, the luxuriance of Ovid and the depth of Shakespeare. And yet it is simple and contains enough to suggest the old Athenian boast of beauty without extravagance."[3]

In justification of the supernatural element in the same play, the French critic, Sylvain Lévi,[4] writes: "The supernatural element which pervades the story threatens to enfeeble the play of human passions and diminish the interest. But Kālidāsa has assigned it a secondary role and almost avoided it except at the denouement in regard to which theory and taste accord in admitting its use.... The gods intervene only in order to unravel the plot."

Similarly, the German scholar Hillebrandt is in raptures over *The Cloud-Messenger,* which he calls "the pearl of Indian lyrics":[5] "In tenderness and beauty of invention as also of the mode of thought, this shortest work of Kālidāsa is unsurpassed. It is difficult to praise too highly either the brilliance of the description of the Cloud's progress, or the pathos of the picture of the wife, sorrowful and alone."

But no tribute can be warmer than the one paid by the American poet-critic, A. W. Ryder: "Poetical fluency is not rare; intellectual grasp is not very uncommon: but the combination has not been found perhaps more than a dozen times since the world began. Because he possessed this harmonious combination, Kālidāsa ranks not with Anacreon and Horace and Shelley, but with Sophocles, Vergil, Milton.... We know that Kālidāsa is a very great poet, because the world has not been able to leave him alone."[6]

These passages are representative enough. In the face of this chorus of foreign praise, it is little wonder that Indians regard Kālidāsa as an incarnation of Sarasvatī, the goddess of poetry, and weave innumerable legends about his life and times. Sri Aurobindo, the sage-critic of modern India declares: "Kālidāsa ranks among the supreme poetic artists with Milton and Vergil and he has a more subtle and delicate spirit and touch in his art than the English, a greater breath of native power informing and vivifying his execution than the Latin poet."[7]

II *His Erudition*

Kālidāsa's erudition deserves special notice. He had a very intimate knowledge of the arts of dancing, music, painting, and sculpture, as evidenced by numerous references.[8] His acquaintance with ancient Vedic lore, law and astronomy, grammar and vocabulary, political science and erotics, religion and philosophy, is equally impressive. Sanskrit poetics, so purist in its attitude and eager to expose the slightest offence to grammar, idiom, reason, and plausibility in poetry is unable to detect a single lapse of the kind in Kālidāsa. Every allusion passes the test of scholarly accuracy as much as of refined literary sensibility.[9] A wedded couple are united like "a base with the affix." A usurper is slain and the rightful king installed on the throne in his stead like "a grammatical substitute in place of root." The efforts of the gods against the demon Tāraka are in vain, "like medicines against an incurable disease." Hanumān jumps across the vast ocean "like an unattached soul crossing the cycle of birth and death." Two friends are in Śakuntalā's train "like the twin stars in the constellation of 'alpha and beta in Libra' following the moon's crescent."

Reference may here be made to the praise heaped upon Kālidāsa by Sanskrit poets and critics. The work of any man of genius is susceptible of endless comment and interpretation, varying as the generations vary from his and from one another. In Sanskrit poetry and criticism, the ideals are cherished universally, and appreciation refers only to commonly shared experience. Kālidāsa's subjects are of eternal interest. To the majority of men and women even today, their own essential preoccupations with love, nature, death, and survival, with the earth, the stars, and the timeless absolute, in no way differ from Kālidāsa's own; and Kālidāsa may still command a willing response from sensitive hearts as he did from the past generations of India:

Who will not delight at the sight of Kālidāsa's fine sayings like honey-laden flower-shoots, so fresh and sweet?

—Bāṇa (c. A.D. 600)

Delightful are Kālidāsa's words as lessons in the art of love, all suggestive, sweet, and captivating like the cuckoo's voice.

—Govardhana (c. A.D. 1200)

After years and years of study, at long last, I feel I have gained entrance into the stream of Kālidāsa's poetry, sweet, limpid and deep.

—Anon.[10]

III *Kālidāsa and Nature*

The attitude of eulogy on the part of ancient critics which we saw in the previous section is not shared by many modern scholars. For example, Dr. P. V. Kane thinks that Kālidāsa suffers in comparison with Bhavabhūti: "In his descriptions of Nature and human feelings, Bhavabhūti is entirely free from conventions. The attitude of other Sanskrit poets (not excluding even Kālidāsa) is generally conventional. They concern themselves chiefly with the cooing of the cuckoo, the mango blossom, the exciting influence of moonlight, the Aśoka and Bakula trees, etc."[11]

There is a general sense in which the very stuff of poetry is convention. As J. L. Lowes puts it: "the very essence of poetic truth is accepted illusion. And illusion, in turn, grows inevitably out of the limitations of the poet's medium. And illusion to which we consent, with all that implies, is the taproot of the conventions of poetry.[12] In this sense Bhavabhūti is as conventional as Kālidāsa."

On the other hand, a warm compliment is paid by A. W. Ryder to Kālidāsa's treatment of nature: "Rarely has a man walked our earth who observed the phenomena of living nature as accurately as he, though his accuracy was of course that of the poet, not that of the scientist. Much is lost to us who grow up among other animals and plants; yet we can appreciate his 'bee-black hair,' his Aśoka tree that 'sheds his blossoms in a rain of tears,' his river wearing a sombre veil of mist, although her reeds seem hands that clutch the dress to hide her charms: . . . his picture of the day-blooming water-lily at sunset":

> The water-lily closes, but
> With wonderful reluctancy;
> As if it troubled her to shut
> Her door of welcome to the bee.[13]

Both these views appear to miss the essence of Kālidāsa's poetry, in as much as they regard his treatment of nature apart from his poetry. This tendency is also noticed among those who compare Kālidāsa's treatment of nature with that of Wordsworth or Keats. This is to miss the central unity of tone in all his writing. Kālidāsa's works are all of a piece and are, in the true Indian tradition, averse to divisions such as the natural, the human, the supernatural.

Kālidāsa may have followed poetic conventions (*kavisamayas*) in matters of detail; but he initiated whole traditions in every literary form he attempted. He is the only poet in Sanskrit who conceived of nature, though symbolically, as the central concern of most of his works, poetic as well as dramatic. Viewed in this light, the cloud becomes the "hero" of his poem *Meghadūta,* a guide, philosopher, and friend to Indra in heaven and the *Yakṣa* on earth, one who is kindness personified, uniting parted couples in love, whether human or not. The range of this metaphor is indeed so infinite that it can embrace the poetic aspects of the sun, moon and stars, wind and rain, river and sea, hill and dale, tree and creeper, flower and fruit, birds and animals, fairies and spirits. It is not only that these pulsate with life—a fact noted by almost every sensitive critic of Kālidāsa—but they combine in a higher harmony of love, more spiritual than sensual. Kālidāsa's poetic world is bathed in beauty and steeped in romance; at the same time it suggests powerfully the truth of Vedānta itself seized in terms of beauty.

In Kālidāsa's imagination, every river is bound with the sea in wedlock, and every tree awaits a mate. The mountains and forests are bosom friends of the cloud; the wind and vernal blooms, confederates of Love. The joy of life is felt as much in the anticipation of love as in its fulfillment; nay, more in suffering and sacrifice than in indulgence. Human nature is so inextricably interlinked with nature that to be blind to this joy is no virtue, and to participate in it no vice. Even God, as Kālidāsa conceives Him, is a devotee of pure love, ever in union with his spouse. Even a juvenile work like the *Ṛtusaṁhāra* (The Cycle of Seasons) unrolls the pageantry of nature only in terms of an imagination aglow with the first experience of love. Women and nature are so closely identified that it is almost impossible to know which the poet is speaking of. Nature repeatedly takes on the appearance of a girl. This poem is almost a hymn to the Earth-Mother, to the fruitfulness and beauty of all living things.

It looks as though Kālidāsa held that the deep mystery of nature could be felt by the human heart at three ascending levels of growing consciousness: sensual attraction, ideal sentiment, and spiritual enlightenment. The first has its raptures and frenzies; it becomes purer only by shedding the dross of sensuality in the fire of separation where love is valued for its own sake. The final phase is reached only through spiritual discipline. Kālidāsa's works can be aptly grouped on this basis. The poem *Ṛtusaṁhāra* and the play *Mālavikāgnimitra* represent a delineation of nature in human terms at the first level of love. If the poem confines itself to its ecstasy, the play highlights the complexities and conflicts incidental to it. The characters here are just human, at ground level. The poem *Meghadūta* and the play *Vikramorvaśīya* represent a delineation of nature in human terms at the second level of love. If the poem embodies the unalloyed form of love-in-separation, the play shows the stages of transition from the first level to the second. The main characters in both are superhuman or semi-divine.

The epic *Kumārasambhava* and the play *Śākuntala* represent nature in human terms at the third and highest level of love, which is spiritual. The spiritual discipline undergone by both Śiva and Pārvatī before they could wed, the imperfection of the first, and the inadequacy of even the second, level of love are brought home to us in the epic in the story of Kāma burned down but revived in a bodiless state. All the characters here are divine, even the mountain Himālaya, symbolic of sublime majesty and might of will. Kālidāsa's account of the physical traits of the mountain shades off imperceptibly into a picture of the divine heights of its personality. To realize the full beauty of the epic, one must be soaked in the myths of ancient India as Kālidāsa himself was. In one flash, the poem reveals the identity of truth, goodness, and beauty in the union of Śiva and Pārvatī brought about by sages.

True to the dramatic form, *Śākuntala* presents this same message in the union of Duṣyanta, Śakuntalā, and Bharata by the efforts of sages like Kaṇva and Mārīca on the spiritual plane. The characters, once again, are semi-divine, and we have enlightened sages at the very center. Kālidāsa's art reaches its apex here in identifying Śakuntalā herself as the fairest flower of the penance-grove, and Duṣyanta as a bee that cannot shed his fickleness until he breathes the rarefied spiritual air of heaven. The imagery of the bee and the flower recurs regularly in almost every significant scene of the play; and Kālidāsa concludes with the observation that only the works of the learned who have drunk of the founts of scriptural truth deserve recognition (*sarasvatī śrutimahatāṁ mahīyatāṁ*).

The epic *Raghuvaṁśa,* with its galaxy of heroes and heroines, is equally in line with the scheme outlined above. It begins with a glowing picture of *tapas* on the part of great men like Raghu, Aja, and Rāma. The loves of Aja and Rāma are the highest expressions of the second level of consciousness mentioned above. The poem concludes with the tragic consequences of the passionate and licentious life led by Agnivarṇa, the last of the Raghus. Starting on a high heroic promise, the poem thus ends on a tragic note.

Such an analysis is in strict consonance with the principles of criticism developed in India by the *dhvani* theorists. To take out of their context single lines or verses about the cuckoo or the *Aśoka* blossom and judge them as conventional or otherwise is to lose sight of the unifying *rasa;* and, as we have seen above, Kālidāsa is most original in his delineation of *śṛṅgāra-rasa.* In its context, has not the bird *cakravāka* itself, in the *Śākuntala,* become a symbolic image of the heroine's separation to come? Is not the *Aśoka* tree almost a living character in the play *Mālavikāgnimitra,* testifying as it does to the princely purity of the heroine by blossoming within five nights of her touch and so bringing about the union of the lovers? We need not multiply instances. From the point of view of *rasa-dhvani,* every detail relating to nature in Kālidāsa can be shown to be full of infinite shades of significance. His roseate bowers and ever blooming flowers do not just belong to a well-regulated garden plot; we have enough indications that, when Kālidāsa saw them, his heart had beaten and he had lived.

One example to show the janus-faced art of Kālidāsa in describing nature is from Canto XIII of the *Raghuvaṁśa,* where the confluence of the Gaṅgā and the Yamunā is being described by Rāma to Sītā as they are flying back to Ayodhyā:

> O faultless Sītā mine, of faultless limbs
> See here the holy Gaṅgā's clear wave
> With Jumnā intermix'd of waters blue.
> See Gaṅgā's current broken by her rival.
> It seems a pearly necklace here that's woven
> With emeralds covering it in splendour mixed

And there a lotus chaplet white, set in
With lotuses all blue at intervals;
And there again, a row of flamingoes
From Mānasa, 'midst geese of dark grey wings.
Seems here like grounds with whitest sandal smeared
And yonder there, all beautiful, equals
The splendour of the moonlight 'neath the shade
By darkness lying there variegated;
And yonder autumnal that 'midst them betray
A little sky to view thro' openings clear;
And here it looks a part of Śiva's form,
Anointed pure with sacred ash all o'er,
And adorned too with snakes all black; ah, thus
The merging glory of the waters two.[14]

It will not do if we admire or criticize the pictures of the black and white presented here as separate and disconnected in themselves. The merging waters have called forth from the poet images of a pearl necklace, a lotus chaplet, a flight of birds, ornamental leaves, moonlight and shade, the clouds, Lord Śiva himself. If we are sensitive *sahṛdayas*, we must see the thread that knits them all, the vision that sees the whole truth in one moment of beauty. If Kālidāsa had not solved the Great Equation, how could he, and by what convention, have connected the birds and the lotuses and Śiva?

IV *Kālidāsa and the Problem of Evil*

"Admirable as is Kālidāsa's work, it would be unjust to ignore the fact that in his dramas and in his epics he shows no interest in the great problems of life and destiny. . . . Assured, as he was, that all was governed by a just fate which man makes for himself by his own deeds, he was incapable of viewing the world as a tragic scene, of feeling any sympathy for the hard lot of the majority of men, or appreciating the reign of injustice in the world. It was impossible for him to go beyond his narrow range." Such is the verdict of Keith,[15] authority on Sanskrit literature. A recent attempt at revaluation undertaken by H. W. Wells in his book *The Classical Drama of India* puts the accent on what he calls "equilibrium" as the essence of Sanskrit plays, a factor "habitually overlooked in Western criticism and in the East, presumably at first taken for granted and later allowed to rest largely unnoted." From this new standpoint it emerges that "the Indian playwright desires neither the more harrowing depths of tragedy nor the irresponsible hilarity of pure comedy. His ideal implies a phase of the serenity to which the deeper spirit of Asia has from its most venerable traditions been dedicated (p. 53). Also "... while the Western drama delights in surprises and looks outward, Sanskrit drama takes the opposite course. Its content is psychological and spiritual rather than social, ethical and intellectual; it aims to etablish the felicity of equilibrium in the soul of each spectator" (p. 32).

Equilibrium, as Indian drama reveals it, is exemplified both in the conception of the plots and, what is more important, in the execution of detail (p. 50). Lest we should belittle the originality of the discovery by equating it with the Indian theory of *rasa,* Mr. Wells adds: "In each play there is observable not only a pervasive sentiment or *rasa,* concerning which the critics have much to say, but a persistent and readily observable equilibrium with which the same critics seem to have been much less consciously concerned" (p. 54).

Did Kālidāsa ignore the problem of evil as urged by Keith, or did he, representing the contemplative East, achieve "equilibrium between opposites" as averred by Wells? An answer to these questions is attempted here in the light of the Indian theory of *rasa.*

While the full significance of the master key of "equilibrium" which would unlock all the secret vaults of Sanskrit drama is not clear, we would be on firmer ground in dealing with the assessment of Keith. Wells's formula of equilibrium is apparently applicable alike to plot and character, style and structure, meaning and message. We are concerned here only with the last aspect, and that too with reference to Kālidāsa.

To the West, life is a riddle and death a mystery. A playwright, whose task is to mirror life, may either go deep and present the tragic quality of the human situation, or may stop at the surface in amusement at the petty life interests of common men. A dramatist's greatness is to be measured only in one of these ways, and it has been well said that "the world is a comedy to those who think, and a tragedy to those who feel." Tragedy is deeply concerned with the problem of evil and man's struggle with destiny; it asserts man's strength in heroic suffering itself. Comedy puts the accent on zest for life with all its oddities and attractions. Judged from this standpoint, Kālidāsa's plays would naturally appear deficient, since his range is restricted to romance. Yet Keith hardly does justice to Kālidāsa when he concludes that Kālidāsa leaves the problem of evil untouched because he was assured that all is governed by a just fate.

The Indian doctrine of *Karma* has been much misunderstood, and its importation into literary criticism is a mistake. *Karma* is the solution proposed by Hinduism to absolve God of the charges of cruelty and partiality in explaining the inequities found in His creation. Never has it been utilized by our classical poets and playwrights to explain away the problem of evil. All our epic heroes are intensely aware of the existence of evil, within and without, and rise manfully to fight it. They all have their share of acute suffering; they struggle, each in his own way, against inexorable fate, instead of succumbing to it passively as "just." Kālidāsa, truly representing the Indian epic tradition, has not forgotten to emphasize this, and his heroines Urvaśī and Śakuntalā suffered because of perverse fate (*pratikūladaiva*) in spite of their innocence. But it will be asked: "Did they not passively submit to it instead of actively resisting it?" The answer lies in a direction but dimly noticed by literary critics; and that is Kālidāsa's idea of the curse (*śāpa*) which bridges two worlds as envisaged by the Indian playwright, the material and the spiritual, and makes for tragic irony.

While most Western plays move in one world of reality, Kālidāsa's heroes and heroines (except in the light *Mālavikāgnimitra*) are simultaneously denizens of two worlds. While Western tragedies end in awe and pity, with only some counsel of despair, the serious drama in Sanskrit rises higher and ends in a hope for humanity, though in a dreamland. True, fate cannot be countered in this life by man; but fate too might relent hereafter if man enlists the sympathy of spiritual sages and gods. This hope follows as a corollary from the Indian faith in births, past and future. Kālidāsa's *Śākuntala* is a real tragedy on the earthly level; the happy ending arrives only in heaven; it has nothing to say about the final happiness of the lovers on earth. In the same way, the tragic madness of Purūravas after his desertion by the celestial nymph is the hard reality on earth, their final reunion being no more than a happy accident occasioned by divine interference. Kālidāsa inherited a literary tradition inextricably bound up with the mythological tradition; hence his attempt to write epics and major dramas involving two planes of existence. The menace of death is mitigated but not underrated on the earthly plane. Shorn of mythology, Kālidāsa's heroes and heroines reveal something akin to the tragic view of life, fully alive to unmerited suffering on earth owing to adverse fate. The Indian theory of *rasa* states unmistakably that the happy ending must be brought about only by supernatural agencies adroitly devised by the poet (cf. the dictum: *kuryānnirvahaṇe 'dbhutaṁ* ["the ending of a play shall perforce include an element of the supernatural"]), indicating that it was no more than a sop to sentimental spectators. Undue emphasis on this literary device appears to have led to the misjudgment of Kālidāsa by Keith.

Let us turn to the motif of the curse. It is something that pursues almost every one of the heroes and heroines of Kālidāsa, in his plays as well as in his poems. Dilīpa and Daśaratha, Urvaśī and Indumatī, Śakuntalā and Duṣyanta—all come under the inexorable effects of a curse. A curse is only a concretisation of *karma* immediately productive; and, more often than not, *karma* is a dereliction of man's duty to spiritual personages or an unconscious misdeed. It partly explains the suffering of man as due to his conscious or unconscious offenses against the moral order, and is in a way another palliative offered to the sentimental playgoers that they might be able to witness the acute suffering of heroic characters without too much anguish. At the same time, the curse cannot wholly explain suffering. It operates usually over a specific period of time, thus keeping the door open for hope from the heavenly quarter. But neither the sop nor the palliative can blind us to the essentially tragic vision which runs through all Kālidāsa's works. He does not ignore evil or death; he only attempts to take away their sting in a way that differs from the Western way.

This leads to the second explanation, proposed by Wells, that Kālidāsa is achieving Asian "poise" or "equilibrium" in his major plays through stories of separation ending happily. The above remarks about Keith's opinion apply with equal force to this seemingly acute observation. This view also exaggerates the importance of the happy ending; what is more, it underestimates Kālidāsa's detailed treatment of love before marriage and gives the same importance to separation as to reunion, so as to make the principle of "equilibrium" neatly applicable. It appears, however, that the core of the play is suffering; and it cannot be bracketed with the happy close which is no more than a *coup de théâtre*. Kālidāsa's philosophy of life cannot be judged according to formulas. It is more akin to Confucius' answer to a man who ventured to ask him about death: "While you do not know life, how can you know about death?"

What is the meaning of life according to Kālidāsa? The question appears to have been ignored by both Keith and Wells. And yet, Kālidāsa has not left us in the dark about it. His exclusive attention to the treatment of love in all its aspects is a sure indicator of his stand. According to him, to love best is to live best. What starts as physical attraction grows into a union of minds and hearts, ripening into spiritual union only after a period of hard trial during separation. Earthly love ends in marriage, as in the *Mālavikāgnimitra*; but heavenly love has to brave severer tests, as in Kālidāsa's other plays, and its highest point is represented in the union of Śiva and Pārvatī over the ashes of Kāma for the divine purpose of creation. The Indian householder's life, with its joys and sorrows, is glorified by Kālidāsa; and he deliberately keeps himself aloof from the tumultuous passions that surge outside that sphere. It must be admitted, therefore, that Kālidāsa's attitude to death and suffering is also restricted to this narrow range; but it does not detract from the universality which is Kālidāsa's unique achievement in his limited range. Nor does it follow (as we shall see in the concluding section) that "he was incapable of feeling any sympathy for the hard lot of the majority of men."

The idea of fate was different in India from that which prevailed in Greece. In Greece, fate was a mysterious, inexorable power which governed men and human events, and from which it was impossible to escape. In India, fate was rather an inevitable consequence of actions done in births antecedent to one's present state of existence, and was thus linked with the doctrine of transmigration. A misfortune was for the most part a punishment, an expiation of ancient faults not yet entirely canceled. In this religio-philosophical explanation of suffering which Kālidāsa and other poets adopted in their works, the problem of evil is not bypassed but recognized. It leads the creative Indian artist to give a new vision of the human station distinct from the tragic vision of the Greeks, yet equally entitled to respect.

When the innocent Sītā in the *Raghuvaṁśa* is forsaken by the ruler Rāma and, unable to endure her sorrow, when she seeks the refuge of mother-earth; when Śakuntalā in the play is deserted by Duṣyanta for no fault of her own and passes years and years in silent suffering; when Pārvatī fails to win the hand of Śiva by her ravishing beauty alone; when Ratī sees her darling love reduced to ashes in the fury of Śiva; when Aja loses his beloved Indumatī by the touch of a floral wreath and when Urvaśī is turned into a creeper, her lover raving in madness; when Mālavikā the princess is reduced to a servant-maid for a whole year; when the fisherman is beaten for a ring he did not steal—we see Kālidāsa's philosophy of life. In his vision, suffering is the rule of life, not the exception.

We might misjudge Kālidāsa's vision of life if we do not realize that in the last analysis, literature itself is a convention. Action in drama or epic takes place in a fictitious world which is not the everyday world. But in this world of imagination we find distilled all thought and emotion of the real world itself. The world of Kālidāsa's imagination is a universalized world, more consistent and more of a piece than the real one. And in this, suffering stands out as the lot of humanity, as the challenging test to try the worth of men and women in life.

That jealousy, hatred, wickedness, and evil are rooted in human nature is never ignored by Kālidāsa. He inherited and openly subscribed to the religious creed that three prismatic qualities, each involved in the other, constitute the human personality: Darkness (*tamas*), Passion (*rajas*), and Goodness (*sattva*). When the first and the second preponderate over the third we have the demonic nature; if they are subordinated to goodness we get the saintly person. Kālidāsa's heroes and heroines are deliberately selected to represent the godly specimens of humanity so that they might serve as models of conduct. They accept life with all its sufferings keeping the goal of final emancipation in view. Nonetheless, when Kālidāsa allows lower characters as representatives of the ordinary run of humanity into his ideal world, like the policemen in the *Śākuntala,* he leaves us in no doubt about the empire of evil in the material world. His *Raghuvaṁśa* is nothing if not a record of the inevitable degeneration in man consequent on swerving from the ideal.

Though Kālidāsa is not oblivious of archetypal conflict rooted in the human nature, it is quite true that he did not despair and did not paint it in lurid colors like other poets in different times and climes. He sees eternity as man's natural condition, not despair. In Kālidāsa's age the poet combined in himself the role of prophet, legislator, and myth-maker. He ventured on generalizations and major pronouncements in the spirit of his time; but, unlike other Sanskrit poets, he spoke also of his own personal experience in his lyrics and plays.

His works are valuable even today because they contain such personal insights besides the platitudes of his own age. Kālidāsa is great because of his intuitions. There is always a gap between traditional formulation of values and individual experience, and across that gap sparks the poetic insight. The transparent placidity of his emotions, his struggles to make terms between this world and the next, his endeavors to reconcile dream, science, and common sense, his faculty for allaying torment by music—these make Indian critics indulge in rhapsodies of praise when speaking of Kālidāsa. We have in him the best thought of the ancient civilization of India couched in beautiful language. His is the wisdom of a sage in explaining the mystery of existence, man's responsibility toward the deity, the difference between good and evil, and the relations between universal good and changing morals.

The Vedāntic dream for perfection, the yearning toward the absolute, the aspiration to oneness and wholeness and organic unity, was the fountainhead of the poetry of Kālidāsa as it was of the contemporary philosophical schools. What we have in Kālidāsa's poetry and drama thus is only an answer in literary terms to the problem of evil with philosophical implications. From Kālidāsa it emerges clearly that man himself is accountable for his pain. The *Śākuntala* may be symbolically regarded as a searchlight turned on man's eternal conflict between ignorance and wisdom, partial knowledge and partial forgetfulness.

One last point remains; and that is about Wells's complaint, quoted at the beginning of this section, against the Indian theorists of *rasa*. He talks of "a pervasive sentiment or *rasa* concerning which the critics have much to say." In fact, no Indian theorist has ever said that *rasa* is only "a pervasive sentiment." They have always held that a play is a unity in a diversity of eight or nine *rasas,* and that the *rasa* underlying throughout is the principal one (*aṅgi-rasa*) while the others contribute to its total effect as ancillaries (*aṅga-rasa*). Whenever they talk of the principal *rasa,* they always imply the existence of other *rasas* beside it.[16] This, too, comes near "the equilibrium of opposites."

Rightly understood and applied, the theory of *rasa* can lead to a proper appreciation of Sanskrit drama. We have to content ourselves here with a random example from the *Śākuntala.* The theory of *rasa* governs at once the nature of the characters and the structure of the play. The "rules" demand that the plot have five "stages" (*artha-prakṛtis*), of which the last, as already noticed, involves a deus ex machina. The first is but preparatory; the second introduces new threads which complicate the main story. The third, called "patākā" (the "Flag"), provides for a new episode in the story, and the fourth envisages minor incidents (*prakarī*); both these are distantly, but deftly, connected with the main theme. It is in these that the playwright has an opportunity of going out of his main story for a while and admitting "the hard lot of the majority of men," with their *rasas* serving as foils even to the main *rasa.* When Kālidāsa takes his heroine to Heaven and dwells at length on the spiritual atmosphere, there we have the *patākā,* breathing tranquillity and pathos, which are perhaps opposed to love, the dominant sentiment of the play. But when we are on earth with a fisherman caught by the police, we have occasion to see Kālidāsa's observation of common humanity. These have only an incidental value, no doubt, from the point of view of the total tone; but they contribute no less to the unfolding of the total meaning of the drama.

Having imbibed the Vedāntic wisdom of India, Kālidāsa was always conscious of *mokṣa* as the highest value. Yet, as a true poet, he depicted it only with reference to the supreme God—Śiva; none of his other characters are motivated in their youthful lives by this quest after perfection. All of them are busy in the pursuit of values well within the reach of our common humanity. Each one of them is imperfect, coming to grips with unavoidable fate and suffering in his own way. Kālidāsa is not oblivious of suffering, but he does not lose hope. His message to man torn between joy and suffering is a lesson drawn from nature:

> On one side the Moon sets behind the Western mount, and on the other the Sun comes to view in all his red glory. By the simultaneous downfall and rise of the two luminaries the people are counseled, as it were, in their vicissitudes of fortune.

It is for us to pause and consider whether Kālidāsa's message is narrower or broader than that of the Western poets.

V *Kālidāsa's Style*

By Kālidāsa's time, a number of devices had been prescribed in books on rhetoric to turn ordinary language into a fit medium for poetry. Simile, metaphor, paradox, paronomasia, and the like, were classified as figures of thought; alliteration, rhyme, and so on, were figures of sound. Several qualities of style like sweetness, brilliance, and lucidity had been set forth as illustrating varieties of poetic diction. The dominant emotions and moods had been explored and explained. What distinguishes Kālidāsa from other Sanskrit poets is his discriminating and imaginative use of these technical devices. He is always their master, never their slave. In him, they appear not as superadded ornaments but as direct expression of feeling laden with symbolic significance.

As noted by Sir William Jones two centuries ago, "the Sanskrit language is of a wonderful structure, more perfect than Greek, more copious than Latin and more extensively refined than either."[16] Its vocabulary is adapted to poetic usage, and its grammar is perhaps the most formal. Everything can be denoted by scores of words, each with a different affective shade; and a new coinage for a new shade of meaning is quite permissible. For example, there is not only the word *Megha* to denote a "cloud," but many combinations of two words meaning "water" and "bearer"; for example, *toya-vāha, ambu-vāha, vāri-vāha,* and so on. Similarly, with "bearer" replaced by "giver," there are more words, like *toya-da, ambu-da, vāri-da, jala-da,* to mean "Cloud." A coinage like *stanayitnu,* meaning "thunderer," will also serve. In the hands of poets, this possibility has been so exploited that there are hundreds of words for "earth," "air," "sea," "water," and so forth. Kālidāsa's special gift lies in choosing the aptest among the numerous possibilities.

Compounds represent another special feature of the Sanskrit language. That which needs a dozen or more English words can be packed into a single word in Sanskrit. To take a random example, Kālidāsa uses *āphalodayakarmaṇām* to mean "they were kings who did not swerve from their appointed duty until they had attained their object."

Nor is this all. The harmony of Sanskrit measures is at once lyrical and majestic. Even today most of them are sung in the classical style of music. Only readers of the Sanskrit original can appreciate Kālidāsa's technique of versification which abounds in subtle rhythms and assonances. For instance, the stately meter, *Mandākrāntā,* employed for *The Cloud-Messenger,* is a quantitative measure of seventeen syllables with two difficult spondees at the beginning and two caesuras in the middle, calculated to express the elegiac mood, as in the line:

— — — — ◡ ◡◡ ◡ ◡ — — ◡ — — ◡ — —
mandaṁ mandaṁ || *nudati pavana-* || *ścānukūlo yathā tvāṁ* ||

The number of meters in Sanskrit is very large; but Kālidāsa, with sound taste, selected only a score or so for his use. In this, too, he set the model for all later generations.

Only a very rough idea can be given of the kind of poetic imagery in which Kālidāsa excels. There is an artificial and decorative use of simile and metaphor in which later Sanskrit poetry abounds; but a very spontaneous and illuminating use is instanced only in Kālidāsa. Recognition of a real or imaginative unity in apparent diversity, and the revelation of this fundamental harmony is the specialty of a creative artist. Words become images of an experience, the rhythm echoes the emotion, and similes embody a thing imaginatively conceived. Speaking of Shakespeare, Gray remarked: "Every word in him is a picture." This is equally true of Kālidāsa. His images are lyrically emblematic and refreshingly original. Personification of natural objects springs from minute observation, and these combine with fancies and conceits derived from mythology and tradition to produce the unique Kālidāsian image.

To take but one random example, even the hackneyed comparison of the moon with a woman's face is handled by Kālidāsa with originality. Queen Sudakṣiṇā, going to the hermitage with King Dilīpa, is "like the conjunction of the star Citrā with the moon." Here the allusion is to the full moon in the first month of spring, the moon representing the king. When King Duṣyanta is reunited with Śakuntalā, he remarks that his condition is like that of "the moon reuniting with the star Rohiṇī after an eclipse." Here, again, the full moon alone is meant; but the star changes into Rohiṇī because, in Indian mythology, though all the stars are supposed to be wives of the moon, Rohiṇī alone is his darling. Similarly, Śiva and Pārvatī are mutually in love, like "the river Gaṅgā flowing into the Sea and the Sea lingering at her mouth."

In the traditional judgment, Kālidāsa is the "king of similes." The superlative praise calls for examination. A poem has its being on at least three levels of reality—the world of the senses, the world of imaginative symbolism, and the world of emotion. The three enter into relation with one another to form the stuff of poetry. It is Kālidāsa's unique command of simile that invests even a trite theme with limitless emotive overtones and symbolic significance. In his handling, the very distinction between art and nature fades away, each running into the other imperceptibly. Talking of *Śākuntala,* a modern critic observes: "Well spiced with delicate and descriptive poetry, the comedy is a delightful amalgam of all the resources of a courtly playwright who makes artifice look natural and nature seem artifice."[18] Though this is true of the entire poetic output of Kālidāsa, the *Śākuntala* provides perhaps the best example of the many levels simultaneously touched by Kālidāsa's imagery.

The play proper opens with a minute description of a deer in flight, running more in the sky than on earth, away from the hunter-king of the city to a serene peace in the sage Kaṇva's calm retreat. The poet remaks that the sight recalls "Lord Śiva with the hunter's bow giving chase to the deer-star." The constellation Orion, pursued as it were by another constellation looking like an archer with a drawn bow, invests the particular deer with heightened significance which unrolls itself gradually as the play progresses. The deer is spared by the hunter despite his zest for hunting, in deference to the hermits' plea that it belongs to their hermitage. But the deer leads to the deer-eyed belle Śakuntalā. Śakuntalā is akin to the deer of the hermitage in guilelessness, simplicity, and ebullient spirits. The deer is her alter ego. Unafraid, the young deer eats grains from her hand and drinks water in the leaf-cup held by her; but runs away in fright from the presence of the king. When the time arrives for Śakuntalā's journey to the city, the deer follows her fondly and clings to her feet and has to be forcibly pushed away. During the trial scene, it is this story of the deer which Śakuntalā relates in the last bid to revive the king's memory of their days of courtship.

If the deer represents the unsuspecting woman who suffers for no fault of hers, the sophisticated man is represented by the image of the bee which recurs in the play at significant points. "The summer flowers worn on their hair by women are half-sucked by bees," we are told in the Prologue. To flit from flower to flower is their nature. The esthete, too, turns to fresh conquests, new pastures. The bee lives in the present and forgets its past diversions. So is the king rebuked by one of his queens while introducing the central theme of forgetfulness in the play.

But Kālidāsa's hero is more than a bee; he has reserves of moral value and spiritual strength. His whole personality and equipment are geared to destroy the enemies of peace, whether they be mad elephants trampling down the hermitage or demons terrorizing the hermits and the gods. He is positively on the side of good, and if he appears evil, it is just a temporary phase, the result of a short-lived curse.

When we dwell on the combined significance of the whole idyllic setting of the play strewn with such expanding images, we realize how Kālidāsa is offering a solution of the very "burthen of the mystery" that is man. Kālidāsa's faith in the essential goodness of man, in the moral order itself, is asserted through the shifting illusions of the reality. Underneath the shifting sands of physical passion, with all its raptures and agonies, the poet sees the steady flame of wisdom which insures peace. The deer is not always hunted; it is spared when taken over by sages and can outgrow its timidity. The bee does not always flit and sting; unwittingly, perhaps, it is on an endless quest for ultimate repose. The phase of forgetting will give place to the phase of remembrance, not only of surface experience but of the foundational reality. In Kālidāsa, external beauty which is sensuous thus becomes an echo of the beauty in man's emotions and shades off imperceptibly into the beauty of the spirit. This unique blend of images working at different levels is the hallmark of Kālidāsa's art and cannot be had in the work of any other Sanskrit poet. Kālidāsa's similes are integral to the theme and add richness and variety by opening new horizons of experience. Unlike the ordinary run of poets, Kālidāsa was able to bring within the compass of his epics an astounding range of experience—literary, mythological, geographical, and religious.

The whole epic, *The Birth of the War-God,* may be regarded as a grand symbolic image of the poet's vision of reality. The myth of the mountain's daughter wedding Śiva is so transfigured in Kālidāsa's imagination that it becomes an epic of the beautiful seeking to wed the ugly. Śiva is ugliness incarnate in his outer form and behavior, just as Pārvatī is an embodiment of supreme beauty. In the poet's philosophy, goodness (Śiva) wears the mask of ugliness which can be removed only by the piercing eye of divine beauty. Beauty and ugliness, which conflict on the mundane level, meet in harmony and become one at the highest level of realization. Such a spiritual realization demands penance and asceticism on the part of both beauty and ugliness. In another sense—and this is the highest Vedāntic wisdom—all beauty is *māyā,* or illusion, a fleeting shadow of the constant Reality. They are always together, and the play of the world goes on so long as the illusion spins out the world's play for the joy of the silent witness, the Reality. But by ascetic contemplation, the illusion itself may turn inward and discover its oneness with the one Reality which never moves or acts, and then the magic show comes to an end. The realized soul will no longer be bound by the trammels of passion and ignorance, but be free. Though his actions in the world continue as before, their sting is removed, and he is on the side of light dispelling darkness without effort.

The above philosophy was well known to Kālidāsa through the *Gītā* and the *Upaniṣads*. But to make the myths and legends of the land a poetic symbol of that perennial philosophy was an achievement which was given only to Kālidāsa to realize. It was said of Socrates that he brought philosophy down from heaven to dwell among men. Similarly, it could be said of Kālidāsa that he brought the Vedāntic wisdom and the religious truths out of the Scriptures to dwell in courts and playhouses. "The way of being in this world while not being of it," is thus the very core of Kālidāsa's religion so ably portrayed in his image of Śiva and Pārvatī.

Talking of Milton's style, F. R. Leavis observes that "he exhibits a feeling for words rather than a capacity for feeling through words." It may be asserted of Kālidāsa's style that both these are harmoniously blended. If it does not possess Shakespeare's colloquial ease, linguistic daring, and unique power, it has elegance and grace, majesty and melody, metrical harmony and richness of overtone, possible only in a refined classical language like Sanskrit. The derivative and traditional elements in the repertory of a court poet are transformed to yield fresh meanings in Kālidāsa's handling of them. His ear for metrical harmony can be brought out by an example; the first line of his invocation in *Urvaśī Won By Valour* reads:

— — — ∪ ∪ — ∪ — ∪ ∪ ∪ —
vedānteṣu || *yamāhurekapuruṣaṁ* ||
— — ∪ — — ∪ —
vyāpya sthitaṁ rodasī ||

The three long syllables at the beginning set the tone, and the successive longs punctuated by shorts maintain the loftiness to the end with assonances that reveal a master's touch.

But when, in the *Śākuntala,* the pursuing king is to be stopped from shooting the deer before it is too late, a different measure is adopted, bristling with many shorts, to add briskness and movement:

∪ ∪ ∪ ∪ ∪ ∪ — —
na khalu na khalu bāṇaḥ
sannipātyo'yamasmin . . .

VI *Kālidāsa as a World Author*

What is Kālidāsa's place when compared with other established world authors? Since the days of Sir William Jones, Kālidāsa has been repeatedly described as the Shakespeare of India. No one disputes their several greatness; but when the comparison is carried into detail to cover the range of vision, the quantity of output and the wealth of imagery, Shakespeare seems to surpass Kālidāsa. Who can deny that Shakespeare's range embraces every human situation, every shade of human feeling, from the darkest to the brightest? The dark forces that sway the human breast receive a penetrating treatment in Shakespeare which we miss in Kālidāsa. Shakespeare's plays certainly outnumber Kālidāsa's three, and Shakespeare's dramatic poetry is so charged with imagery that one might say we witness in him a rebirth of the English language. Shakespeare's characters represent all walks and stations of life, and his sympathy extends as much to the low as to the high. Kālidāsa's characters have an unmistakably aristocratic bias.

Admitting all this and much more, still, if Kālidāsa bears comparison at all with Shakespeare, it is because of his merits after shortcomings have been discounted. Unlike Shakespeare, Kālidāsa has a universal system of philosophy and a broad practical religion that act as both frame and reference. If Shakespeare's wrestle with the problem of evil led him, through a maze of bloody murders and dark witchcraft, to "a dark period" when he seems to have lost faith in humanity until he recovered it in the gossamer fairylands of his last plays, we see in Kālidāsa a sustained faith and understanding which comes to terms with evil itself, a wisdom which is serene and steady, a confident and certain progress toward the goal of peace. Shakespeare's characters, like Hamlet, reflect the Jacobean age of doubt in transition from medieval ideas to the new Copernicanism which shook the foundations of faith. But Kālidāsa, inheriting the Vedāntic wisdom, has a firm faith which is proof against all doubts. While Shakespeare wrestles with opposites to find a balance for himself, Kālidāsa is aware all the time of the norm of truth from which errors are but departures. Shakespeare went down into the depths of his being and hung over abysses to the point of madness and yet groped back to truth. But Kālidāsa was clear from the beginning about the various corridors of illusion that veil reality. He confined himself to the presentation of one master passion—love, in all its various manifestations—till he reached, by way of it, the infinite values of beauty, truth, and goodness. On the other hand, we have Kālidāsa excelling in poetic genres which Shakespeare never essayed.

Thus viewed, Shakespeare and Kālidāsa may complement each other, each lacking what the other possesses in perfection, and each meriting therefore the world's equal attention. Kālidāsa's message of peace, cultivated as a value, alongside his religion of beauty, secures him a place beside Shakespeare.

Kālidāsa's integrated personality, esthetic temperament, and religious faith are best seen in his women characters—all sweet and beautiful, guileless and good. There is no place in them for a Lady Macbeth or a Goneril and a Regan. The Indian poet has no interest in "cuckoldom," a recurring subject in Shakespeare. Perhaps the only play of Shakespeare which comes close to Kālidāsa's in portrayal of love is *Romeo and Juliet.* Hamlet leaves Ophelia to avenge the death of his father; while listening to the voice of Desdemona, Othello is still thinking of the sound of battles; but Romeo, like Agnimitra and Purūravas, forgets everything in his overmastering passion. Juliet alone perhaps unites in herself that mixture of qualities that we find in Śakuntalā; hardly Imogen, hardly Cordelia.

Another play which has offered critics a close parallel between Shakespeare and Kālidāsa is *The Tempest.* We have a preponderance of poetry in *The Tempest* as well as in *Śākuntala.* The setting of nature plays an equally important role in both. In both, magic and the supernatural forces operate. The contrast between the island and city life in the one is similar to the contrast between the hermitage and the palace in the other. But as pointed out in a recent study, "conflict for Shakespeare is the essence of the play, and harmony is always superficial and precarious. While for Kālidāsa it is the harmony within the rhythm of life that is the essence of play and conflict is but a peripheral skirmish."[19] Both stand out in combining sublimity with pathos, bitterness with joy, love with peace, delirium with inspired wisdom, and sensuousness with seriousness. Similarly, Shakespeare's narrative poems bear comparison with Kālidāsa's *Meghadūta* and *Ṛtusaṁhāra.*

It would be interesting to compare Kālidāsa with Goethe, who, as we have seen, was an admirer of Kālidāsa, and was influenced no less by Shakespeare. Goethe has been described as "the greatest European man of letters of the Romantic Age," and the term "world literature" was invented by him.[20] In Matthew Arnold's words, he was "Physician of the iron age." His whole life was an unceasing quest for wisdom "between the infinities of music and metaphysics." Kālidāsa bears close resemblance to him in this respect, since both have the widest interests. Goethe's teaching has been styled the creed of culture. This creed of self-development is the main theme of Kālidāsa too. The same universal, full, and rich humanity we see in both. In point of many-sided genius, again, embracing the lyrical and dramatic modes, they resemble each other. Goethe's philosophy of beauty, like Kālidāsa's, took into account "passionless passion," the world of dreams and the world of things animate. But here the comparison must stop. Kālidāsa does not have Goethe's vision of evil. There can be no likeness in detail between a German apostle of modern culture and an Indian poet who wrote at least fifteen centuries earlier.

The closest parallel to Kālidāsa in point of epic excellence is, however, Vergil, who wrote in Latin, a classical language like Sanskrit. Just as Vergil modeled his literary epic on Homer's primary epic, so too did Kālidāsa introduce innovations in the epic manner of Vālmīki. Just as Vergil, in his *Aeneid,* glorified Rome of the Augustan age, so did Kālidāsa sing in praise of India's golden age ushered in by Vikramāditya. Vergil aimed at showing "that the empire of Augustus was connected with the mythical past by an unbroken chain of human endeavor and divine interposition,"[21] and retold the story of its origins casting a Homeric glamor over the earliest traditions. So did Kālidāsa sing, in his *Dynasty of Raghu,* of the glories of the kings of Ayodhyā tracing their lineage to the Sun-God himself. In point of style also, Vergil and Kālidāsa illustrate equally what Matthew Arnold calls the "grand style severe" in contrast to the "grand style simple" of the primary epic.[22] Again, they are alike in their dread of vulgarity and quaintness and in a genuine feeling for breadth of effect, sententious maxims, and ornate descriptions.

The poetic diction of Kālidāsa is more elegant than that of Vālmīki and at the same time less artificial than that of later court poets like Bāṇa. A single example will illustrate the point. Bāṇa uses mouth-filling compounds and packs his verse with alliterative sound, while Kālidāsa is content with euphonic assonance. Let us see how the two describe their favorite god, Śiva, the moon-crested lord. Bāṇa says:

namastuṅgaśiraścumbicandracāmaracārave
trailokyanagarārambhamūlastambhāya śambhave.[23]

Kālidāsa's diction is more appealing and less bombastic when he writes:

> *aṇimādiguṇopetam aspṛṣṭapuruṣāntaraṁ*
> *śabdamīśvara ityuccaiḥ sārdhacandraṁ bibharti yaḥ*[24]

The same epic meter is used—*anuṣṭubh* is employed by both—but the contrast in effect is vast.

In respect of love lyrics, Kālidāsa's place in Sanskrit poetry is somewhat analogous to that of Ovid, who also started classical models and became the favorite of innumerable poets as well as of the elite of succeeding generations. If we may believe popular legend, both led amorous lives and met with inglorious ends. The reputation of both was carried from court to court, and men of taste were fond of their tags and allusions. Scholars discussed them, poets studied and copied them, and schoolboys construed and memorized their lines. Both make free use of mythology. The quality of sweetness valued by critics is pre-eminently present in both. Both succeeded to an extent in liberating the imagination of the age from the yoke of the moralists and in affirming the autonomy of love. Both fostered a new estheticism highly valued by fashionable poets at royal courts. But Kālidāsa did not, like Ovid, choose disappointed love as his main lyrical theme. He preferred to draw a clear line between the courtesan's love and married love.

Nonetheless, as Griffith sums up so objectively, the melody of Kālidāsa's rhythm, whose sweetness and purity of language are so admirably adapted to the soft repose and celestial rosy hue of his pictures, the grace and beauty that pervade so much of the work must not allow one to deny that occasionally, even in the noble Sanskrit, if we judge him by a European standard, Kālidāsa is bald and prosaic.[25]

We have a recent example of the interpretation of the *Śākuntala* as fundamentally a wish-fulfillment fantasy, arising from a basic Oedipal conflict.[26] We must say that such application of sophisticated taste or psychoanalytical method to Kālidāsa's classics is not likely to yield valuable results. The keynote of Kālidāsa's works is better struck in two oft-quoted Sanskrit verses:

> *yā vyāpāravatī rasān rasayituṁ kācit kavīnāṁ navā*
> *dṛṣṭiryā pariniṣṭhitārthaviṣayonmeṣā ca vaipaścitī*

te dve apyavalambya viśvamaniśaṁ nirvarṇayanto vayaṁ
śrāntā naiva ca labdhamabdhiśayana tvadbhaktitulyaṁ sukhaṁ.

We scanned life with a poet's scrutiny
And thrilled in Beauty's little flickerings,
Then searched with rushlights of philosophy
And roared: "Now stands revealed the core of things!"
Till, O thou Vast, couched in the Primal Ocean
Our hearts surmised in deep world-weariness:
We missed Thy highest boon—the heart's devotion
To thee, a bliss of everlasting Grace.[27]

purā kavīnāṁ gaṇanāprasaṅge
kaniṣṭhikādhiṣṭhitakālidāsā
adyāpi tattulyakaverabhāvād
anāmikā sārthavatī babhūva.[28]

They of yore, in remembering poets, began the count on the little finger with Kālidāsa, the greatest; but in the absence even today of any poet comparable to him, the next remains "unnamed," the *anāmikā*.

We have seen in the course of the book how Kālidāsa appeared on the Indian literary horizon like a new star. Assimilating the rich literary, religious, and philosophical traditions of his land, he broke away from the literary conventions of the past and started new traditions of art-epic and lyric, romantic comedy and tragicomedy. In classical Sanskrit literature, though he was the first to initiate major changes, he held the central place of honor for more than ten centuries. In Sanskrit literary history, there are hundreds of authors under each genre; but none of them contest the undisputed claim of Kālidāsa as the prince of poets in any of the forms he touched. Sanskrit literary theorists who specialize in making a science of literary defects are so overpowered by his genius as to declare that his very lapses are more admirable than the successes of other poets.

The epic and dramatic tradition inherited by Kālidāsa stressed the working-out of an underlying divine purpose in the conflicts of heroes. They were fraught with interest to the nation as a whole. Numerous anonymous authors from all over the country contributed to the growth of the Indian epics into mammoth proportions, though in their nucleus we may see one hand, either Vyāsa or Vālmīki, at work. The Indian people made them the permanent possessions of their minds. They not only enjoyed them but looked to them for their values in life and raised them to the rank of religious books. Kālidāsa, who imbibed the spirit of the timeless epic myths, reduced them to a manageable size and remodeled them into a gay pageant, bright with color and enlivened with music. His poetic personality contributed individuality to his works. His characters were full of life, and his descriptions were both sweet and artistic. The meaningless mixture of the human and superhuman in the early epic gave place to rich human significance in the hands of Kālidāsa.

The emancipation of the human virtues from the magical ones is an important contribution of Kālidāsa. His works may contain some superhuman elements, but they merit our attention even today because of their human interest. The wide range of his themes and their epic magnitude are brought within the bounds of a refined poetic art wherein harmony of sound, mastery of rhythm, the exact and exquisite employment of words become important in themselves. Kālidāsa's sense of formal beauty and excellence is matched only by the grandeur of his conception. For seekers of uniform beauty in language as well as thought, Kālidāsa will always remain the poet of their choice.

Kālidāsa can reflect the deep and solemn emotions of a quiet recluse as well as the guileless whims of a country maid, can describe equally the play of children as well as the wiles of women, the valor of heroes as well as the pranks of jesters. His treatment of love possesses subtlety and penetration. And he has a rare gift for the intrinsic recognition of excellence in man, bird, or beast; in mountain, river, or hill; in bud, leaf, or flower, thanks to his passionate lyrical impulse. The sources of his poetic imagery are as vast as the universe comprising

> heavens, earth, biological and zoological kingdoms, domestic life, family relations, social life, mythology, fine arts, mental states and conventions, poetic or otherwise.[29]

They endow his works with a local color and make the past live in the present.

We need not wonder, then, if Kālidāsa was acclaimed as a master by succeeding generations of poets and critics in India whether they wrote in Sanskrit or Prakrit, Bengali or Kannada, Marathi or Malayalam. The eulogies of Kālidāsa alone coming from later men of letters would form a large volume if a complete collection were made. Kālidāsa has influenced, enriched, and delighted the Indian mind through some twenty centuries, which is not a small achievement. Further, his works are refreshingly free from the recurring motive of second-rate court poets; namely, adulation of the royal patron and begging for his very material favor.

We have also seen how this representative genius of India has his place secure on the canvas of world literature in the judgment of expert critics of the East as well as of the West. Kālidāsa describes not only the beauty, power, and peace of forest retreats,[30] but also the grandeur and glory of royalty illustrating, as it were, the truth of Pascal's saying that "justice without power is impotent, power without justice is tyranny." In more than one work he has brought out that love should be based on more than mere sense thrill. Its spiritual vistas are opened up and its consummation is shown in the growth of family bonds with the child as the center.

The one message underlying all his works is that moral power is moral rightness. At a time when civilization is threatened with extinction by atomic weapons, it is good to remind ourselves that the way to enlightenment is through sorrow and suffering, patience and charity. If in India today even the teeming millions are convinced that love, beauty, and peace are some of the values to be attained in life, it is a pointer to the influence, however remote and indirect, of Kālidāsa on generations and generations of Indians. Kālidāsa has become an integral part of India's national heritage; and he deserves most to become part of international heritage too.

We cannot think of a better conclusion for this study of Kālidāsa than the following considered judgment of one of the earliest orientalists, Christian Lassen: "Kālidāsa may be considered as the brightest star in the firmament of Indian artificial poetry. He deserves praise on account of the mastery with which he wielded the language, and the fine sentiment with which he imparts to it a simpler or more artificial form according to the subjects of which he treats without falling into the later hair-splitting and overstepping of the boundaries of good taste; on account of the multifariousness of his creations, his ingenious invention and happy choice of subjects; on account of complete fulfillment of his poetical intentions; and on account of the beauty of his representations, the tenderness of his feeling and the richness of his imagination."[31]

VII *Epilogue: Kālidāsa and Indian Civilization*

Though authentic Indian chronicles are not available about the civilization of ancient India, Indologists have succeeded in piecing together a dependable picture of Indian life and thought about the dawn of the Christian era. The earliest Aryan settlers of the *Ṛgveda* soon spread themselves from their northwestern home eastward, and mixed even racially with the Dravidian and earlier Austro-Asiatic inhabitants of India, evolving new forms of religion and language by the time of the epics. Śaivism and Vaiṣṇavism were the dominant forms of epic religion coexisting with a number of other religious cults devoted to the worship of the sun, the mother-goddess, Skanda, and so on. The latter were sometimes popularized by foreign settlers like the Persians, Greeks, Bactrians, and Scythians, who had established permanent cultural contacts with India.[32]

We know from Indian history that the Brahmanical religion itself was challenged by two of its offshoots from within: Jainism and Buddhism. These two reformist religions laid great stress on asceticism and nonviolence and received great encouragement from the Mauryan emperors, Chandragupta and Asoka. They saw the rise of a new literature, too, in both Prakrit and Sanskrit.

At the same time, since some provinces like Gāndhāra in India formed, for a considerable period, colonies of the Persians, Greeks, Kushans, Śakas, and so on, in succession, they imbibed the secular values of the foreign civilization also. The very titles of the Indian kings were modeled after the high-sounding Persian titles; administrative and police officers of the state were very often of foreign blood. The Indian court encouraged the cultivation of the fine arts, and we find the birth of new schools in painting, sculpture, and literature.

Kālidāsa's works confirm this general picture of Indian civilization constituted out of various strands, indigenous and foreign. The main contending forces were religious dogma and secularism, asceticism and hedonism, orthodoxy and estheticism. The caste system that prevailed brought its own problems though it helped social solidarity in its own way. On the intellectual side, India produced not only the secular sciences like dramaturgy, erotics, medicine, and metrics in this age but also the philosophical catechisms and law codes. On the literary side, it was left to the genius of Kālidāsa to become a prophet of the new synthesis in the simmering ideas of his age and to give a new status to the Sanskrit language. If Sanskrit came to be recognized as a national language all over the country, it was in no small measure due to the grace and finish that Kālidāsa contributed to it.

Kālidāsa reconciles the cosmic view of the eternal Vedānta with the claims of worldly values and contending religious sects. He is as much a votary of truth as of beauty. Kālidāsa embodies some of the Buddhist ideals of life like compassion and morality in the picture of his ideal kings and shows how they are as much Hindu as Buddhist ideals. Within the limits of his art, Kālidāsa gives expression to free thought, challenging outmoded traditions and superstitions in art, science, and religion. Kālidāsa's social, political, and economic views are also very broad and ahead of his time. He is sensitive to the seeds of decadence luxury carries within itself and is attuned to the lure of the spiritual and the enchantment of Yoga. Kālidāsa thus represents the very best in Indian thought and civilization. Such a flowering of Indian genius we see only once in the Golden Age of Hindu India.

Notes and References

Chapter One

1. Satis Chandra Vidyabhushana refers to Ceylonese traditions that point to a place in Ceylon as the grave of Kālidāsa. See *Proceedings and Transactions of the First Oriental Conference* (Poona: Bhandarkar Research Institute, 1920), p. lix.

2. For a fairly exhaustive list of translations up to 1935, see M. B. Emeneau's *Union List of Printed Indic Texts and Translations in American Libraries* (New Haven: American Oriental Society, 1935), pp. 145-49.

The most readable translation in English of all the works of Kālidāsa is Ryder's. It was first published in London, Dent's Everyman's Library, in 1912, and has been often reprinted, the latest being the Dutton Paperback Everyman reprint of 1959.

3. Some of these are:

   1. Hāla's *Sattasaī*, V. 64.
   2. *Jyotirvidābharaṇa*, an astrological work ascribed to Kālidāsa, XXII. 10.
   3. *Vikramacarita* (translated into English as "Vikrama's Adventures" by F. Edgerton in the Harvard Oriental Series, Vol. XXVI and text Vol. XXVII). See Introduction to Vol. XXVI.
   4. *Kālakācārya-kathā* (edited and translated by W. Norman Brown (Washington: Smithsonian Institute, 1933).
   5. Harisvāmin's *Śatapatha bhāṣya* (Sarasvati Bhavan Library, Benares), Colophon.
   6. *Skānda-Purāṇa,* Kumarikā-khaṇḍa, XL. 5253.
   7. Subandhu's *Vāsavadattā,* translated by L. H. Gray (New York: Columbia University Press, 1913).
   8. Somadeva's *Kathāsaritsāgara,* translated by Tawney under the title *Ocean of Story,* edited by Penzer, London. See Vol. III, pp. 206 ff. and Vol. IX, pp. 43 ff.

4. Sir William Jones, Von Humboldt, Gorresio, and Griffith are the early Orientalists who held this view. Cf. R. T. H. Griffith, *The Rāmāyaṇa of Vālmīki,* Vol. I (London: Trubner & Co., 1870), p. xvii.

Among modern scholars, the following deserve mention:

   1. K. C. Chattopadhyaya, *Allahabad University Studies,* Vol. II, pp. 80-113.

2. K. M. Shenbavanekar, *Journal of the University of Bombay,* Vol. I, pt. 6.
3. R. B. Pandey, *Indian Historical Quarterly,* Vol. XIX, pp. 359-409.
4. T. J. Kedar, *Nagpur University Journal,* December, 1939, etc.
5. J. L. Shah, *Ancient India,* Vol. III (Baroda: Shashikant & Co., 1940), pp. 421-23.
6. Raj Bali Pandey, *The Vikramāditya of Ujjayinī* (Banares: Shatdala Prakashan, 1951).

5. 1. A. A. Macdonell, *History of Sanskrit Literature* (London: Heinemann, 1909), p. 325.
2. A. B. Keith, *History of Sanskrit Literature* (Oxford: Oxford University Press, 1953), p. 82.
3. Massen-Oursel, *Ancient India and Indian Civilization* (London: Kegan Paul, Trench Trubner & Co., 1934), pp. 276-77.
4. M. Winternitz, *A History of Indian Literature,* Vol. III. Fasciculus 1 (Calcutta: Calcutta University, 1959), p. 23.
5. Krishnaswami Aiyangar, "Vikramāditya," *Sir Asutosh Memorial Volume* (Samaddar: Patna, 1928), pp. 143-63. F. W. Thomas, V. A. Smith, H. C. Raichoudhuri, A. S. Altekar, V. V. Mirashi, and other historians also share this view. The main evidence favoring Chandragupta II—Vikramāditya identification is the reference in Rāshṭrakūṭa inscriptions of the eighth century A.D. to Chandragupta's patronage to men of letters. For the original passages, see *New Indian Antiquary,* Vol. II (Bombay: Karnatak Publishing House), pp. 686-87.

6. Viz, Vatsabhaṭṭi's Mandasor Inscription (J. F. Fleet, *Gupta Inscriptions,* No. 18, Corpus Inscriptionum Indicarum, Vol. III, Varanasi Indological Book House, 1963) in which two verses show a clear imitation of the *Cloud Messenger,* II. 1.

7. This theory was first propounded by S. Ray (*Proceedings and Transactions of the First Oriental Conference* [Poona: Bhandarkar Oriental Research Institute, 1920], p. lix). It was accepted by K. S. Ramaswami Sastri in his book, *Kālidāsa* (Srirangam: Srivanivilas Press, 1933), p. 66, and is recently revived by Dr. V. Raghavan (article on Indian [Classical Sanskrit] Literature in J. T. Shipley's *Encyclopaedia of Literature* [New York: Philosophical Library, 1946], p. 451).

8. For a history of ancient Indian cities like Ujjayinī, Vidiśā, and Pāṭaliputra, see H. C. Ray Chaudhuri, *A Political History of Ancient India* (Calcutta: University of Calcutta, 1953), p. 556.

9. A very perceptive exposition of Kālidāsa's *milieu* appears in

Sri Aurobindo's essay on the age of Kālidāsa, included in the booklet *Kālidāsa* (Calcutta: Arya Sahitya, 1929). See also, H. C. Chakladar, *The Geography of Kālidāsa* (Calcutta, *Indian Studies,* 1963).

10. Reference may be made in this connection to the following word picture given by Bhau Daji:

> The "towery summits" of the Himalaya decked with "diadems of snow," the peak of Kailāsa "reflected in the waters of the dark Yamunā," "the rippling Gaṅgā laving the mountain pine," "the musky breezes throwing their balmy odours over eternal snow," "wilds, where eager hunters roam, tracking the lion to his dreamy home," "the peaks where sunshine ever reigns," where "birch trees wave," "the bleeding pines their odorous gums distil," and the musk-deer spring frequent from their covers, "the magic herbs pour their streamy light from mossy caverns through the darksome night," the wild kine "with her bushy streaming hair," the fierce elephant, the startled deer, the lotuses that "lave their beauties in the heavenly Ganges' stream," the mountain-lake, "the clefts from which dark bitumen flowed," the melting snow, the cool gale, the "rude mantles of the birch-tree's rind."
>
> Such are some of the slides shown by Kālidāsa of Himālaya's splendor. *The Literary Remains of Dr. Bhau Daji* (Calcutta: Ram and Friend, 1887), p. 49.

11. E.g., Kṣemendra's *Aucityavicāracarcā,* Rājaśekhara's *Kāvyamīmāṁsā,* Bhoja's *Sarasvatīkaṇṭhābharaṇa* and *Śṛṅgāraprakāśa.* While this Kuntala King is usually identified with the Vākāṭaka King Pravarasena II by all historians, V. V. Mirashi thinks that he is a ruler in the line of Mānāṅka of the Vatsagulma branch. See V. V. Mirashi, *Indological Studies,* Vol. I (Nagpur: Vidarbha Samsodhana Mandal, 1960), pp. 3-11.

12. For a detailed study of Vālmīki's influence on Kālidāsa, see V. Raghavan, "Vālmīki and Kālidāsa," *K. V. Rangaswami Aiyangar Commemoration Volume* (Madras: G. S. Press, 1940), pp. 409-24. See also Dr. Nilmadhav Sen's observations in *The Cultural Heritage of India,* Vol. II (Calcutta: The Ramakrishna Mission Institute of Culture, 1962), pp. 96-97.

13. For a fuller account of this, see Chapter 5 in this book.

14. For a detailed consideration of this question, see Chapter 5 in this book.

15. A very penetrative study of the essentials of Indian poetics can be had in Daniel H. H. Ingalls' *An Anthology of Sanskrit Court*

Poetry (Cambridge, Mass.: Harvard University Press, 1965), Introduction.

16. A fuller discussion of this question appears in R. D. Karmarkar's article, "The Chronological Order of Kālidāsa's Works," in the *Proceedings and Transactions of the Second Oriental Conference* (Calcutta, Calcutta University, 1923), pp. 239-47.

17. For further information, see S. K. De, "Kālidāsa," Louis de la Valle Poussin Memorial Volume, Calcutta, *Indian Historical Quarterly* (1940), p. 170.

Chapter Two

1. For a further account of the *Rasa* theory, see R. K. Yajnik, *The Indian Theatre* (London: George Allen and Unwin, 1933), pp. 29 f.; and K. Krishnamoorthy, *Essays in Sanskrit Criticism* (Dharwar: Karnatak University, 1963), pp. 64-96.

2. We know from Indian history that Puṣyamitra, the commander-in-chief of the last Mauryan king at Pāṭalīputra, beheaded the king and usurped the throne.

3. *Kālidāsa* (Everyman's Library No. 629 [London: J. M. Dent & Sons, 1912]), p. 110.

4. *Ibid.*, p. 114.

5. *Mālavikāgnimitra,* III. 15.

6. A. B. Keith, *The Sanskrit Drama* (Oxford: Oxford University Press, 1954), p. 147; A. W. Ryder, *op. cit.*, p. 109.

7. *Ṛgveda,* X. 95; *Śatapatha Brāhmaṇa* V. 1-12.

8. *Bṛhaddevatā,* VIII. 140-47, *Sarvānukramaṇī on Ṛgveda* X. 85.

9. *Viṣṇudharmottara-, Brahmāṇḍa-, Vāyu-, Viṣṇu-, Bhāgavata-, Devībhāgavata-,* and *Harivaṁśa-* are some of the *Purāṇas* which relate this story.

10. *Matsya* and *Padma.*

11. Cf. Walter Ruben, *Kālidāsa* (Berlin: Akademie Verlag, 1957), p. 70; S. K. De, *A History of Sanskrit Literature* (Calcutta: Calcutta University, 1947), p. 139.

12. Sri Aurobindo, *Kālidāsa* (Second Series) (Pondicherry: The Aurobindo Ashram, 1954), p. 56.

13. Prakrit and Apabhraṁśa are different dialects derived from Sanskrit.

14. *Vikramorvaśīya,* IV. 7.

15. *Ibid.*, VI. 2.

16. *Ibid.*, VI. 28.

17. *Ibid.*, VI. 32.

18. *Ibid.*, VI. 38.

19. A. B. Keith, *The Sanskrit Drama* (Oxford: Oxford University Press, 1954), p. 156.

20. H. H. Wilson, *The Theatre of the Hindus* (Calcutta: Susil Gupta, 1955), p. 64.
21. *Dharma* stands for religious and moral good.
22. Cf. K. P. Kulkarni, *Sanskrit Drama and Dramatists* (Satara: K. P. Kulkarni, 1927), p. 138.
23. One of the best translations available in English with the Sanskrit text is by Monier Williams, 2nd ed. (Oxford: Clarendon Press, 1876). A more recent and close rendering of the Bengali version (Harvard Oriental Series, Vol. 16, Cambridge, Mass., 1922), is by M. B. Emeneau (Berkeley: University of California Press, 1962).
24. Introduction to the stage edition of *Śākuntala* by K. Das Gupta and L. Binyon (Calcutta: Macmillan, 1920).
25. Quoted in *The Literary Remains of Dr. Bhau Daji* (Calcutta: Ram and Friend, 1887), p. 1.
26. See General Introduction to the *Vikramorvaśīya of Kālidāsa* (New Delhi: Sahitya Akademi, 1961), p. xxvii.
27. The story also occurs in the *Padmapurāṇa* which closely follows Kālidāsa's play. Many scholars feel that the Purāṇa version is based on the play. Talking of the epic version itself, N. K. Sidhanta writes: "Śakuntalā's story has been supposed to be a later addition; neither the matter nor the form has anything common with the main parts of the story. The theme is one of romantic love which rarely plays a part in heroic stories. The full and ambitious descriptions of natural scenes and surroundings remind one more of the works of a later age, of the dramas of Kālidāsa and others." N. K. Sidhanta, *The Heroic Age of India* (London: Kegan Paul, Trench Trubner & Co., 1929), pp. 74-75. This supposition is not tenable. It is admitted as a genuine part of the original epic even in the Critical Edition of *The Mahābhārata* published by the Bhandarkar Oriental Research Institute, Poona.
28. *Śākuntala*, ed. S. K. Belvalkar (New Delhi: Sahitya Akademi, 1965), I. 3.
29. *Ibid.*, I. 4.
30. *Ibid.*, I. 15.
31. *Ibid.*, I. 17.
32. *Ibid.*, III. 12.
33. A. B. Gajendragadkar, *The Abhijñāna-Śākuntala* (Surat: Popular Book Store, 1950), p. 530.
34. G. C. Jhala, *Kālidāsa—A Study* (Bombay: Popular Book Depot, 1949), pp. 186-87.
35. *Op cit.*, IV. 6.
36. *Ibid.*, IV. 9.
37. *Ibid.*, IV. 19.
38. *Ibid.*, IV. 18.

39. *Ibid.*, V. 5.
40. *Ibid.*, V. 6.
41. Quoted by C. R. Devadhar and N. C. Suru in their edition of the play (Bombay: Booksellers Publishing Company, 1948), Introduction, p. xviii.
42. For further details see "Śakuntalā—Its Inner Meaning," *A Book of Indian Culture*, ed. D. S. Sarma (Calcutta: Macmillan, 1944), pp. 1-8.
43. *Ibid.*
44. *Śākuntala*, VII. 12-13.
45. See M. Winternitz, *History of Indian Literature*, Vol. III (Calcutta: Calcutta University, 1959), p. 214.
46. Sri Aurobindo, *Kālidāsa* (Second Series) (Pondicherry: Aurobindo Ashram, 1954), p. 5.
47. *Ibid.*, p. 73.

Chapter Three

1. Cf. "Purāṇas and the Rāmāyaṇa were in existence when Kālidāsa composed the *Raghuvaṁśa*. Yet he followed the Purāṇic version in the portion of the genealogy that he gives which is common to both." F. E. Pargiter, *Ancient Indian Historical Tradition* (London: Oxford University Press, 1922), p. 121. According to this writer, the Purāṇas are anterior to Kauṭilya who alludes to them and belong to the fifth century B.C. *Loc. cit.*, pp. 54-55.
2. R. Tagore, *Creative Unity* (Calcutta, Macmillan, 1959), p. 53.
3. Sri Aurobindo, *Kālidāsa* (Calcutta: Arya Sahitya Bhavan, 1929), pp. 23-24.
4. A. B. Keith, *History of Sanskrit Literature* (Oxford: Oxford University Press, 1948), p. 87.
5. For instance, Ānandavardhana, of the ninth century, who wrote the *Light of Suggestion in Poetry*. An English version of this work by K. Krishnamoorthy is published in the Poona Oriental Series (1954).
6. *Kumārasambhava*, VII. 63.
7. Sri Aurobindo, *Kālidāsa*, 2nd ed. (Pondicherry, Sri Aurobindo Ashram, 1950), pp. 48-49.
8. T. G. Mainkar, *Kālidāsa, His Art and Thought* (Poona Deshmukh Prakashan, 1962), pp. 95 f.
9. A. B. Keith, *History of Sanskrit Literature* (Oxford: Oxford University Press, 1948), p. 94. Cf. also B. C. Mazumdar, Journal of the Royal Asiatic Society, London, 1909, pp. 731 f.
10. R. D. Karmarkar, *Kālidāsa* (Dharwar: Karnatak University, 1960), p. 77.

Chapter Four

1. The latest scholars who have written monographs on *Kālidāsa, viz.*, Walter Ruben and R. D. Karmarkar (already referred to), do not mention the *Ṛtusaṁhāra*. The two recent verse translations of the lyric are by R. S. Pandit (Bombay, 1947); and Shankar Mokashi Punekar (Bombay, 1966). For details see Selected Bibliography.

2. *Kālidāsa, op. cit.* (quoted in the flyleaf of S. M. Punekar's translation referred to in note 1.) The only evidence strongly pointing to Kālidāsa's authorship of the poem is: (1) Vallabhadeva, in his *Subhāṣitāvalī* (c. A.D. 1500), an anthology of quotations, cites two verses (VI. 17 and 20) from the poem as Kālidāsa's. (2) An inscription of A. D. 473 contains a few verses modeled on the *Ṛtusaṁhāra*, without, however, mentioning the author. Even if our poem is spurious, it cannot be dated later than the fifth century A.D.

3. Preface to Rooke's English translation of the *Meghadūta* (London: Oxford University Press, 1935).

4. Quoted in Ruben's *Kālidāsa*. See Selected Bibliography.

5. Quoted in *The Literary Remains of Bhau Daji* (Calcutta: Ram and Friend, 1887), p. 7.

6. V. V. Mirashi, *Kālidāsa* (Marathi) (Nagpur: Vasudev Vishnu, 1934), pp. 39-40, 113 f.

7. S. K. De's edition, *Meghadūta* (New Delhi: Sahitya Akademi, 1957).

Chapter Five

1. Max Müller, *A History of Ancient Sanskrit Literature,* p. 3; Upnekat and Bagvedam stand for Upaniṣads and Bhāgavataṁ.

2. *Loc. cit.*, pp. 1-57.

3. This extract is taken as quoted in C. K. Venkataramiah's *Kālidāsa* (Kannada) (Bangalore, Government of Mysore, 1966), p. 4.

4. Sylvain Lévi, *Le Théâtre Indien* (Paris: E. Bowillon, 1890), p. 175.

5. Hillebrandt, *Kālidāsa* (Breslau: M. & H. Marcus, 1921), pp. 69 f.

6. Ryder, *Shakuntalā and other Writings* (London: J. M. Dent & Sons, 1912), pp. xx-xxi.

7. Sri Aurobindo, *The Foundations of Indian Culture* (New York: Sri Aurobindo Library, 1953), p. 337.

8. Monographs have been written setting forth in detail Kālidāsa's reference to the arts and sciences. See Sivaramamurti, *Sanskrit Literature and Art,* "Memoirs of the Archaeological Survey of India," No. 73, 1955; S. A. Sabnis, *Kālidāsa* (Bombay: Tripathi, 1966); B. S. Upadhyaya, *India in Kālidāsa* (Allahabad: Kitabistan, 1949).

9. Cf. Haridas Sinharay, "The Rhetorical Devices in Kālidāsa," *Indian Studies,* Vol. IX. No. 2 (Calcutta, 1961), pp. 133-36.

10. Quoted in the anthology, *Subhāṣitaratnakoṣa,* Harvard Oriental Series, Vol. 42 (1963), p. 296.

11. P. V. Kane's edition of *Uttararāmacaritam* (Bombay: Oriental Publishing Company, 1916), Introduction, p. x.

12. J. L. Lowes, *Convention and Revolt in Poetry* (London: Constable & Co., 1930), p. 3.

13. A. W. Ryder, *Shakuntalā and Other Writings of Kālidāsa* (London: J. M. Dent & Sons, 1912), pp. xi-xii.

14. Translation Griffith's. See Selected Bibliography.

15. *The Sanskrit Drama,* p. 160. See Keith in Selected Bibliography.

16. *Ekaḥ kāryo rasaḥ sthāyī rasānāṁ nāṭake sadā*
rasastadanuyogitvādanye tu vyabhicāriṇaḥ
—*Saṅgītaratnākara,* VII. 1682.

17. Sir William Jones, *Asiatic Researches,* Vol. I (London: John Murray, 1798), p. 422.

18. J. Gassner, *Masters of the Drama,* 3rd ed. (Dover, 1954), p. 120. Quoted by Jordens in the article described in note 19 below.

19. Joseph T. F. Jordens, "Idyll and Reality in the Shākuntala and the Tempest," *Jadavpur Journal of Comparative Literature,* Vol. 5 (1965), pp. 1-21.

20. J. B. Priestley, *Literature and Western Man* (London: Heinemann, 1960), pp. 129-33.

21. Routh, *God, Man and Epic Poetry* (Cambridge, England: Cambridge University Press, 1926), p. 205.

22. *Matthew Arnold,* ed. John Bryson (London: Hart Davis, 1954), p. 320.

23. *Harṣacarita,* I. 1.

24. *Kumārasaṁbhava,* VI. 75.

25. R. T. H. Griffith, *The Birth of the War God* (London: W. H. Allen & Co., 1853), p. ix.

26. *Approaches to the Oriental Classics,* ed. Bary (New York: Columbia University Press, 1959).

27. Translation by Dilip Kumar Roy, *Golden Jubilee Souvenir* (Tiruvannamalai: Sri Ramanasharma, 1949), p. 119. Text of verse as quoted in Ānandavardhana's *Dhvanyāloka* (Bombay: Nirnayasagar Press, 1935), pp. 284-85.

28. An oft-repeated traditional saying.

29. P. K. Gode, *Studies in Kālidāsa* (*Proceedings and Translations of the First Oriental Conference* [Poona: Bhandarkar Oriental Research Institute, 1920]), pp. 204 ff.

30. Cf. "Kaṇva's hermitage is surely not far from the forest of

Arden," A. L. Basham, *The Wonder that was India* (London: Sidgewick & Jackson, 1954), p. 440.

31. Quoted in *The Literary Remains of Dr. Bhau Daji* (Calcutta: Ram and Friend, 1887), p. 2.

32. Cf. Benjamin Walker, *Hindu World,* 2 vols. (London: George Allen & Unwin, 1968). Articles on Śakas, Greece, Kālidāsa and so on.

Selected Bibliography

PRIMARY SOURCES

1. *Texts*:

The number of editions in which Kālidāsa's works, either wholly or in part, are available in India are too numerous to be catalogued. Practically every linguistic region has its own editions in the regional scripts, not to speak of Devanāgarī editions which have an all-India currency. Since Kālidāsa is a most studied author in Indian schools and colleges, several modern editions with annotations in English and modern Indian languages have appeared, but their scholarly value is not very great. Only the most reputed and widely used editions are recorded below, at least one for each text:

Kālidāsa-Lexicon. Vol. I, Pt. I-III. Ed. A. Scharpe. Brugge, Rijksuniversiteit te Gent, 1954-58. The most recent, authoritative and critical edition of the text of all Kālidāsa's works in Roman script. It comes handy for non-Indian readers who may not be familiar with the Devanāgarī and other scripts employed in Indian editions of Kālidāsa.

The Mālavikāgnimitra. Ed. K. P. Parab. Bombay, Nirnayasagar Press, 1935. Edition most referred to by scholars; contains an old Sanskrit commentary by Kāṭaya Vema which explains difficult words and offers illustrations from the text for the rules of Sanskrit drama.

The Vikramorvaśīya. Ed. H. D. Velankar. New Delhi, Sahitya Akademi, 1965. By far the most scholarly edition available setting out at length variant textual readings in the critical apparatus. The editor's Introduction is exhaustive and discusses ably the several problems of textual and higher criticism.

The Abhijñāna-Śākuntala. Ed. S. K. Belvalkar. New Delhi, Sahitya Akademi, 1965. Decisive in fixing the most authentic recension of the play by a comparison of many manuscripts belonging to different versions. Does not have any informative Introduction.

The Abhijñāna-Śākuntala. Ed. A. B. Gajendragadkar. Surat, Popular Book Store, 1950. Most popular in Indian schools and colleges, giving as it does a detailed Introduction, a complete English translation, and extensive notes, grammatical, mythological, and critical.

The Raghuvaṁśa. Ed. W. L. Pansikar. Bombay, Nirnayasagar Press, 1916. Dependable text accompanied by the well-known Sanskrit commentary of Mallinātha, deservedly honored in traditional studies of Kālidāsa.

The Kumārasambhava. Ed. W. L. Pansikar. Bombay, Nirnayasagar Press, 1927. Contains Mallinātha's commentary on the first eight cantos besides a reliable text.

The Ṛtusaṁhāra. Ed. V. R. Nerurkar. Bombay, The Oriental Publishing Company, 1966.

The Meghadūta. Ed. S. K. De. New Delhi, Sahitya Akademi, 1957. Contains the most up-to-date constitution of a critical text. It also carries a very exhaustive Introduction discussing the origin and development of the genre of *dūta-kāvya* in Sanskrit literature and the number of commentaries written on Kālidāsa's text. Those interested in Mallinātha's commentary and English explanations may see M. R. Kale's fifth edition of the *Meghadūta,* Bombay Booksellers' Publishing Co., 1956.

2. *Standard English Translations*:

Numerous translations by Indian authors have been attempted of the plays and poems of Kālidāsa, since they are often prescribed as textbooks for study in school and college courses. Most of them confine themselves to literal and mechanical renderings in what may be called Indian English. They are left out of account here as mostly inelegant and unrewarding. Only standard English translations which have a higher literary aim and which have won the applause of Western readers are included in the list below:

Mālavikāgnimitra. Translated into prose by C. H. Tawney. 2nd ed., Calcutta, Thacker Spink, 1891. This prose translation is very close to the original and readable at the same time.

Vikramorvaśie or *The Hero and the Nymph.* Translated into verse by Aurobindo Ghosh. Calcutta, Sri Aurobindo Pathamandir, 1911. The esteemed author, also an English poet, recaptures the spirit of the Sanskrit play in English verse. The English lines have force, majesty, and grace. But it is more a liberal rendering than a literal translation.

Śakoontala or *The Lost Ring.* Translated into prose and verse by Sir Monier Monier-Williams. Hertford, Stephen Austin, 1894. By far, this is the best and most widely known of all English translations of Kālidāsa's *Śākuntala.* Its popularity is evidenced by the numerous editions into which it has run. This translation combines dignity of expression with close adherence to the original text.

Kālidāsa, Translations of Shakuntalā and Other Works. By A. W. Ryder. London, J. M. Dent & Sons, 1912. While Ryder's translation of *Shakuntalā* is complete, we have only translations of select portions of other works by Kālidāsa. This translation has won the plaudits of readers of varied tastes all over the world. The rhymed verse and chiseled prose of Ryder succeed most in expressing Kālidāsa's subtle shades of mood and feeling. No other translator has achieved the same measure of success. Yet he, too, takes liberties with Kālidāsa's text, and at times his diction appears overornamented. Ryder's Introduction reveals how warm and genuine is his appreciation of Kālidāsa's genius.

Raghuvaṁśa or *The Story of Raghu's Line.* Translated into verse by Johnstone P. De Lacy. London, J. M. Dent & Sons, 1902. This is a free and elegant rendering. But it is long out of print and difficult to procure.

Kumārasambhava or *The Birth of War-God.* Translated into verse by R. T. H. Griffith. London, W. H. Allen & Co., 1853. All the merits and demerits of Victorian English verse are illustrated in this verse rendering. It is heavy and high-sounding and yet succeeds in reflecting Kālidāsa's noble thoughts and power of expression better than many others.

Ṛtusaṁhāra or *The Pageant of the Seasons.* Verse translation by R. S. Pandit. Bombay, National Information, 1947. The Indian translator was equally at home in Sanskrit and English and this is a highly poetic lyric, but the gain in glitter contrasts with the simple charm of the original.

Ṛtusaṁhāra or *The Cycle of the Seasons.* English verse equivalents by S. M. Punekar. Bombay, Sigma Publications, 1966. This is the latest attempt by an Indian professor to give verse-to-verse translation. The English versification reveals competence though at times the expression is stilted.

Meghadūta or *The Cloud-Messenger.* Translated into prose by King Charles. London, John Murray, 1930. The English prose here is almost poetic in appeal and is eminently successful in recapturing the grace and force of Kālidāsa's Sanskrit.

Idylls from the Sanskrit, containing translations from the Raghuvaṁśa. By R. T. H. Griffith. Allahabad Pāṇini Office, 1912. *Specimens of Old Indian Poetry.* Containing translations from *Śakoontala,* "Summer" (from the *Ṛtusaṁhāra*) and the "Messenger-Cloud." By R. T. H. Griffith. Allahabad, Pāṇini Office, 1914. Both of these are random renderings of only parts of Kālidāsa's works. The author's classical learning is evident in his scholarly poetic versions; but they have not won popular praise. They may not appeal to modern taste.

SECONDARY SOURCES

AUROBINDO, SRI. *Kālidāsa.* Calcutta, Arya Sahitya, 1929. This is a short essay attempting to appraise the achievement of Kālidāsa against the background of Vālmīki and Vyāsa who ushered in epic poetry in India. It is a penetrating and illuminating study of trends in Sanskrit literature.

BHAVE, S. S. *Kālidāsa.* Baroda, Good Companions, 1942. In this monograph we have a general Introduction to Kālidāsa's works and a detailed study of the *Meghadūta* in particular. An English translation of some paragraphs of appreciation of this poem from Hillebrandt's German book on Kālidāsa is also appended.

CHAKLADAR, H. C. *The Geography of Kālidāsa.* Calcutta, Indian Studies, 1963. The book contains a detailed account of the various cities, mountains, rivers, etc., of geographical interest mentioned in Kālidāsa's works.

GARRETT, JOHN. *Classical Dictionary of India.* Madras, Higginbothams & Co., 1871. Contains information on all myths and legends in Sanskrit epics and Purāṇas.

HILLEBRANDT, A. *Kālidāsa.* Breslau. M. & H. Marcus, 1921. The first monograph on the poet and his works written in German; contains discussions about the author's date besides summaries and critical appreciation of the works.

JHALA, G. C. *Kālidāsa, a study.* Bombay, Popular Book Depot, 1949. An analytical study and appreciation of Kālidāsa's works designed for the general reader.

KARMARKAR, R. D. *Kālidāsa.* Dharwar, Karnatak University, 1960. The lectures delivered by the author on Kālidāsa are brought together here in book form. They embody the considered opinions of the learned author on controversial problems regarding Kālidāsa's date and the sequence of his works in addition to interesting literary estimates.

KEITH, A. B. *The Sanskrit Drama.* Oxford, Oxford University Press, 1925; *A History of Sanskrit Literature.* Oxford, Oxford University Press, 1948. These two books are the standard works of reference on the history of Sanskrit drama and Sanskrit poetry, respectively. They embody the results of modern research on questions of chronology and provide short critical estimates of all important works. A study of these is indispensable for understanding the place of Kālidāsa in the history of Sanskrit drama and poetry. But Keith is hypercritical at times in estimating Indian traditional opinions.

KONOW, STEN. *Das Indische Drama.* Berlin, Verleger, 1920. A thoroughgoing documentation of European studies of Sanskrit drama and dramatists is a speciality of this work in German. Its literary analyses and estimates are, however, cursory.

LÉVI, SYLVAIN. *Le Théâtre Indien.* Paris, E. Bowillon, 1890. Besides a detailed analytical account and literary appreciation of the different Sanskrit plays, this work in French furnishes authoritatively and understandingly the main features of Sanskrit dramatic theory.

MACDONELL, A. A. *A History of Sanskrit Literature.* London, Heinemann, 1909. One of the pioneer attempts at acquainting the general reader with an outline of Sanskrit drama and poetry with select illustrations in English translation. Though addressed to the general reader, it has not sacrificed academic precision. It may be read with interest and delight even today. Space devoted to Kālidāsa in this book is naturally limited.

MAINKAR, T. G. *Kālidāsa, his art and thought.* Poona, Deshmukh Prakashan, 1962. A new theory about the identity of Kālidāsa with Īśvarakṛṣṇa, the celebrated author of the *Sāṅkhyakārikā* is provided in this recent monograph. It also includes interesting analytic-critical studies of all the individual works.

RAJA, C. K. *Kālidāsa.* Waltair, Andhra University, 1956. These lectures, delivered to university students now released in book form, present a very individualistic and diffuse consideration of Kālidāsa and his works. Several of the views do not bear scrutiny; nonetheless, it provides a good introduction to a study of Kālidāsa from the traditional Indian standpoint.

RAPSON, E. J. (ed.). *History of India.* Vol. I, Cambridge, England, Cambridge University Press, 1922. Regarding questions of Indian chronology, the views embodied in this history will be found most objective and reliable. It contains also useful observations on the political, social, and religious conditions in the different periods of ancient Indian history.

RUBEN, WALTER. *Kālidāsa.* Berlin Akademie, 1957. This German scholar's monograph subjects Kālidāsa's works to a new examination from what appears to be a Marxist view of literary progress and finds the Sanskrit poet deficient on several counts. It is thought-provoking.

SHEKHAR, I. *Sanskrit Drama.* Leiden, Brill, 1960. In this recent research publication, we have new theories propounded of the origins of Indian drama. Kālidāsa's plays are subjected to a comparative examination.

WELLS, H. W. *The Classical Drama of India.* Bombay, Asia, 1963. For a very discerning and illuminating presentation of Sanskrit dramatic theory in comparison with other theories developed in

China, Japan, and elsewhere, this book is invaluable. It also provides a fresh criticism of Kālidāsa's plays along with others.

WILSON, H. H. *The Theatre of the Hindus*. Calcutta, Susil Gupta, Reprint: 1955. (First published: London, 1837 under the title: *Hindu Theatre*.) Represents the earliest Western attempt to present the broad features and characteristics of Sanskrit drama; the extensive work of Wilson is only reprinted here in part; some more recent contributions on the subject are included instead. We see in Wilson's work the first reactions of Western readers to Sanskrit plays.

WINTERNITZ, M. *A History of Indian Literature*. Vol. III. Fasciculus 1, Calcutta, Calcutta University, 1959; Part I, Delhi, Motilal Banarsidas, 1963. These are the English translations of parts of the monumental work of Winternitz in German. While the first fasciculus treats of poetry, Part I relates to drama. The treatment in both is exhaustive, sympathetic, and scholarly. Perhaps the most widely read of all histories of Indian literature to date.

Index